Welcome to the world heritage ci

D1686033

There are places that somehow manage to get under your skin, even though you don't really know them all that well. Bruges is that kind of place. A place made for people. A city whose history made it great, resulting in a well-deserved classification as a Unesco World Heritage site.

In this guide you will discover Bruges' different facets. There are five separate chapters.

In **chapter 1**, you will read about the ten *must see* sights and get a brief summary of the city's history. After that, you will immediately set off to explore the most beautiful places in Bruges during three inspiring walks. The detailed **map of the city** – which you can simply fold out of the back cover of this guide – will make sure that you don't lose your way.

Chapter 2 provides a summary of the many different possibilities for exploring Bruges and gives details of everything the city has to offer in cultural terms: a calendar of the most important events and a complete summary of the Bruges museums, attractions and other sites of interest, including historical, cultural and religious buildings and locations. Bruges' beautiful squares and enchanting canals are the regular backdrop for top-class cultural events. And few cities have such a rich and diverse variety of museums, which

cʌ .... primitives and beautiful lace work to the finest modern art of today. Further in this chapter, gourmets will be delighted by our summary of award-winning restaurants and shopaholics by our tips for authentic and high-quality shops and stores.

Bruges is a city with a lot to offer. In **chapter 3**, a number of 'outsiders' who found their way to Bruges and stayed, tell you why they love the city so much. They also reveal their favourite addresses for a bite to eat (from classy restaurants to trendy eateries), a glass to drink or a little bit of relaxing shopping.

Staying a bit longer in the region? **Chapter 4** suggests a number of excursions to the other Flemish historical cities, the Bruges' wood- and wetlands, the coast and the Westhoek.

Are you just dying to explore Bruges? In **chapter 5** we will give you all the practical info and tips you need to prepare for your visit.

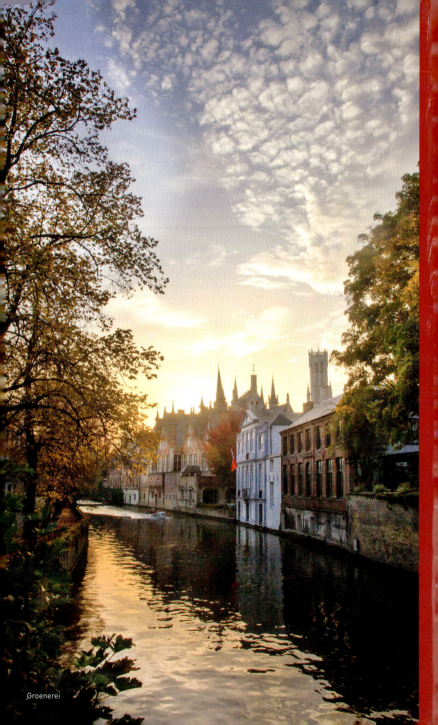
Groenerei

Discover
Bruges

History in a nutshell

The Market Square in Bruges, 17th century
(painting by Jan-Baptist Meunincxhove)

Water played a crucial role in the birth and development of Bruges. At the place where the city was first born, a number of streams flowed together to form a river (the Reie), which then ran northwards through the coastal plain. Through a series of tidal creeks, the river eventually reached the sea. Little wonder, then, that even as far back as Roman times there was already considerable seafaring activity in this region. This has been proven by the discovery of the remains of two seagoing ships from this period, dating from the second half of the 3rd century or the first half of the 4th century. Even so, it would be another five centuries before the name 'Bruges' first began to appear – the word being a derivative of the old-German word 'brugj', which means 'mooring place'.

Bruges' growing importance also resulted in it becoming the main fortified residence of the counts of Flanders, so that from the 11th century onwards the city was not only a prosperous trading metropolis, but also a seat of considerable political power.

Taking off

When the city's direct link with the sea was in danger of silting-up in the 12th century, Bruges went through a period of anxiety. Fortunately, the new waterway of the Zwin brought relief. As a result, Bruges was able to call itself the most important trade centre of Northwest Europe in the following century. The world's first ever stock exchange ('Beurs' in Dutch) was also founded in Bruges. These market activities took place in the square in front of the house owned by a powerful local family of brokers, the Van der Beurse family. As a result, their name became linked for all time with this kind of financial institution. In spite of the typical medieval maladies, from epidemics to political unrest and social inequality, the citizens of Bruges prospered, and soon the city developed a magnet-like radiation. Around 1340, the inner city numbered no fewer than 35.000 inhabitants.

The golden century

The success continued. In the 15th century, Bruges' golden century, business was better than ever before. The Burgundian dukes rebuilt and enlarged their residence in Bruges and the production and sale of luxury goods reached new heights. Famous painters such as Jan van Eyck and Hans Memling – the great Flemish primitives – found

their creative niche here. The fine arts flourished, and in addition to wonderful churches and unique 'nation houses' (embassies), the monumental town hall was also completed. Bruges' success seemed imperishable.

Decline

The sudden death in 1482 of the much-loved ruler, Mary of Burgundy, heralded the start of new and less fortunate times for the city. The relationship between the citizens of Bruges and their lord, the widower Maximilian of Austria, turned sour. The Burgundian court left the city, with the international traders following in its wake. Long centuries of wars and changes of political power took their toll. By the middle of the 19th century, Bruges had become an impoverished city. Strangely enough, its fortunes were changed for the better by the writing of a novel.

Revival

With great care, Bruges took its first steps into tourism. In *Bruges la Morte* (1892), Georges Rodenbach aptly describes Bruges as a somewhat sleepy, yet extremely mysterious place. Above all, the 35 photographs included in the book made its readers curious about what they might find. Soon Bruges' magnificent patrimony was rediscovered and its mysterious intimacy turned out to be its greatest asset. Building on this enthusiasm, the city was provided with a new seaport, which was called Zeebrugge. The pulling power of Bruges proved to be a great success and UNESCO added the medieval city centre to its World Heritage list. The rest is history.

From early settlement to international trade centre (...-1200)

- **851** Earliest record of the city
- **863** Baldwin I takes up residence at Burg square
- **1127** Charles the Good, Count of Flanders, is murdered in the Church of Saint Donatian; first town rampart; first Bruges city charter
- **1134** Creation of the Zwin – evolving from the Sincfal marshes – that links Damme with the sea

Bruges' golden century (1369-1500)

- **1369** Margaret of Dampierre marries Philip the Bold, Duke of Burgundy. Beginning of the Burgundian period
- **1384** Margaret succeeds her father Louis of Male
- **1430** Marriage of Duke Philip the Good to Isabella of Portugal; establishment of the Order of the Golden Fleece
- **1436** Jan van Eyck paints the panel *Madonna with Canon Joris van der Paele*
- **1482** Mary of Burgundy dies as a result of a fall with her horse
- **1488** Maximilian of Austria is locked up in Craenenburg House on Markt for a few weeks

851 **1200** **1300** **1500**

Bruges as the economic capital of Northwest Europe (1200-1400)

- **1245** Foundation of the Beguinage
- **1280** Reconstruction in stone of the Belfry after the destruction of its wooden predecessor
- **1297** Second town rampart
- **1302** Bruges Matins and Battle of the Golden Spurs
- **1304** First Procession of the Holy Blood
- **1376-1420** Construction of the City Hall

The city gets her second wind (1500-1578)

- **1506** The cloth merchants Jan and Alexander Mouscron buy Michelangelo's *Madonna and Child*
- **1528** Lancelot Blondeel designs the mantelpiece of the Liberty of Bruges
- **1548** Birth of the scientist Simon Stevin
- **1562** Marcus Gerards engraves the first printed town map of Bruges
- **1578** Bruges joins the rebellion against the Spanish king

An impoverished town in a pauperised Flanders (1584-1885)

1584 Bruges becomes reconciled with the Spanish king

1604 The Zwin is closed off

1713-1795 Austrian period

1717 Foundation of the Academy of Fine Arts, which formed the basis for the collection of the Groeninge Museum.

1795-1814 French period

1799 Demolition of Saint Donatian's Cathedral and renovation of Burg

1815-1830 United Kingdom of the Netherlands

1830 Independence of Belgium; birth of Guido Gezelle

1838 First railway line in Bruges inaugurated on 't Zand

The new city (1971-...)

1971 Amalgamation Law incorporates former suburbs

1985 King Baudouin opens new sea lock at Zeebrugge

2000 Historic city centre is given World Heritage status; Euro 2000 (European Football Championship)

2002 European Capital of Culture

2008 *In Bruges* is released worldwide in cinemas

2009 The Procession of the Holy Blood is granted Intangible Cultural Heritage status by UNESCO

2013 Bruges is the setting for the Bollywood blockbuster *Peekay*

2016 Bruges' De Halve Maan Brewery opens the first underground beer pipeline in the world.

1600 **1700** **1800** **1900** **2000**

Provincial town with revived ambitions (1885-1970)

1887 Unveiling of the statue of Jan Breydel and Pieter de Coninck (Markt)

1892 Publication of *Bruges la Morte* by Georges Rodenbach

1896 Start of the construction of the seaport

1897 Dutch becomes the official language

1902 First important exhibition of the Flemish primitives

1914-1918 The Great War: Bruges is a German naval base

1940-1945 The historic city centre survives Second World War almost unscathed

1958 First Pageant of the Golden Tree

The highlights of Bruges
The 10 classic places
that no one should miss!

🚤 Rozenhoedkaai and the Bruges canals, a typical city view

The Rozenhoedkaai (Rosary Quay) links the Belfry with the city's network of canals, the true 'veins' of Bruges, and offers a unique and picturesque panoramic view. Hardly surprising, then, that the Rozenhoedkaai is the most popular photographic hotspot in town! You can discover many more special places and hidden gems during a boat trip on the canals. From the water, Bruges is even more enchanting. A classic that you really don't want to miss.

🐴 Markt, an absolute must

The vibrant centre of the city has been dominated for centuries by the 83-metre high Belfry. Today, you can climb right to the top of this impressive tower. You will be rewarded with a spectacular view of Bruges and the surrounding countryside. The Markt (Market Square) is also home to the Historium, a top attraction that takes you back in time to the city's medieval past. Surrounded by colourful houses, the Market Square is also the regular standing place for the famous horse-drawn carriages. *(Read more on pages 56 and 63-64)*

Medieval splendour on the Burg

The Burg is the beating heart of the city. From the 14th century town hall, which is the oldest in the Low Countries, Bruges has been governed for more than 600 years. This majestic architectural square also contains the Palace of the Liberty of Bruges, the former Civil Registry and the Basilica of the Holy Blood. No other location in Bruges bears greater testimony to the city's former wealth. *(Read more on pages 55, 59 and 72-73)*

Strolling through the old Hansa Quarter

From the 13th to the 15th century, Bruges was the most important trading centre in

North-West Europe. Spanish merchants settled along the Spaanse Loskaai (Spanish Quay) and in the Spanjaardstraat. The Germans or Easterners – 'oosterlingen' in Dutch – took up residence in the Oosterlingenplein. In this old Hansa Quarter, you can admire the mansions of the wealthy international merchants and the great trading nations of the day. You can almost still smell the atmosphere of the Middle Ages.

The Flemish primitives: timeless beauty

In Bruges' golden century – the 15th century – art was a major issue. Leading artists of

the day, like Jan van Eyck and Hans Memling, came to live and work in the city. Today, you can marvel at the masterpieces of the world-famous Flemish primitives in the Groeninge Museum and the St. John's Hospital. Here you can come face to face with the great paintings that were created in the city all those centuries ago.

(Read more on pages 62-63 and 69-70)

Church of Our Lady: a work of beauty in brick

The Onze-Lieve-Vrouwekerk (Church of Our Lady), with its imposing 115.5-metre high brick tower, is not only a fine testimony to the skill of the Bruges master builders of yesteryear, but is also the second tallest brick church spire in the world. Inside, the church visitors will be moved by the magnificence of Michelangelo's white marble *Madonna and Child*. *(Read more on pages 65-66)*

Quiet contemplation in the Beguinage

Some places are so beautiful that they leave you speechless. The Beguinage is just such a place. This is where the beguines – emancipated women who lived pious and chaste lives without taking holy orders – once lived together in harmony. This walled oasis of religious peace, with its delightful inner garden, wind-twisted trees and white-painted gables, can charm even the most cynical of souls with its deafening silence. *(Read more on page 55-56)*

Minnewater: romance all the way

This small rectangular lake was once the mooring place for the barges that sailed the inland waterways between Bruges and Ghent. Nowadays, together with the Minnewater Park, this stretch of water – whose name means 'Lake of love' – is the most romantic spot in the city. The Minnewater Bridge offers magical views over one of the most idyllic places in Bruges.

Concert Hall, or Culture with a capital C

This tall and stately culture temple on 't Zand gives the square its own unique dynamism. In the soberly decorated auditorium, visitors can enjoy classical music and contemporary dance in the best possible setting. During the day, you can explore this remarkable building by following the Concertgebouw Circuit, an original and entertaining experience route that ends with a fantastic view of Bruges from the roof terrace. *(Read more on pages 53 and 84)*

Almshouses: charity embodied in stone

Villages within the city. That's how you can best describe these residential centres, which originated in medieval times and are still occupied today. The almshouses were first founded centuries ago for charitable purposes. Today, with their picturesque gardens, their white-painted gables and their perfect peace and quiet, they are amongst the most tranquil places in Bruges. *(Read more on page 18)*

Walk 1

Bruges, proud World Heritage City

Beguinage

Bruges may be, quite rightly, very proud of her World Heritage status, but the city is happily embracing the future too! This walk takes you along world-famous panoramic views, sky-high monuments and centuries-old squares invigorated by contemporary constructions. One foot planted in the Middle Ages, the other one firmly planted in the present. This walk is an absolute must for first-time visitors who would like to explore the very heart of the city straight away. Keep your camera at the ready!

WALK 1

» START

'z Zand
(Concert Hall)

» DISTANCE

3 km

» FINISH

Saint John's Hospital

•••• Alternative route

13

From 't Zand to Simon Stevinplein

This walk starts at the tourist office **i** 't Zand (Concert Hall).

't Zand is dominated by the Concert Hall **17**, one of Bruges' most talked-about buildings. Clear-cut proof that this World Heritage city isn't afraid of the future. The Concertgebouw Circuit **17** will take you behind the scenes and right to the very top of this magnificent building, where you can find an interactive space for sound art. You can also enjoy the wonderful view over the Bruges skyline. Don't forget to drop in at the tourist office **i** 't Zand (Concert Hall) on the ground floor: here you will find all the necessary tourist information as well as expert advice on all cultural events, and you can buy your tickets immediately.

On pages 120-123 you can learn more about the Concert Hall in an interview with Albert Edelman.

Leave **i** 't Zand (Concert Hall) behind you, walk along the square and turn into Zuidzandstraat, the first street on the right. Saint Saviour's Cathedral **23** looms up ahead on your right after three hundred metres.

Bruges' oldest parish church is located on a lower level than the present Zuidzandstraat, which is situated on an old sand ridge. What's more, in the Middle Ages people simply threw their refuse out onto the street where it was then flattened by passing carts and coaches. This raised the street level even further. Inside Saint Saviour's, the church tower's wooden rafters can be lit. The cathedral treasury displays interesting copper memorial plaques, fine examples of gold and silver and paintings by Dieric Bouts, Hugo van der Goes and Pieter Pourbus.

BURG SQUARE: AN ARCHITECTURAL SYNOPSIS

Art lovers have already noticed that the Burg projects a wonderful cross-section of stunning architectural styles. It is, indeed, a summing-up in one place of all the styles that have caught our imagination throughout the various centuries. From Romanesque (Saint Basil's Church) and Gothic (City Hall) by way of Renaissance (Civil Registry) and Baroque (Deanery) to Classicism (Mansion of the Liberty of Bruges). There's no need to go and dash all around Bruges to see it all!

Turn right before the cathedral into Sint-Salvatorskerkhof. Walk around the cathedral and take the fourth street on the right, the Sint-Salvatorskoorstraat. This will take you to the Simon Stevinplein. This attractive square, lined with cosy restaurant terraces in summertime, is named after Simon Stevin, a well-known Flemish-Dutch scientist. His gracious statue naturally takes centre stage.

Markt and Burg

Continue down Oude Burg, a street in the right-hand corner of the square. Before long you will see the Cloth Halls **09** on your left. These belong to the Belfry **05**. You're allowed to cross the halls' imposing inner courtyard between 8.00 a.m. and 6.00 p.m. during the week, and between 9.00 a.m. and 6.00 p.m. on Saturday. Markt is at the other end of the courtyard. If the gate is closed, turn back and walk down Hallestraat, which runs parallel to the Halls.

Walk 2 (see pages 25-27) comments more extensively on Markt.

Return to the Belfry **05** and walk down Breidelstraat, a traffic-free alley on the corner at the left. Continue to the Burg square.

Along the road on your right you will notice De Garre, a narrow alley. This may be the narrowest street in Bruges (try walking side by side here!), it nevertheless boasts a fair number of cosy cafés. The Burg is the most majestic square in the city, so take your time to admire its grandeur. The main character in this medieval story is the City Hall **08** **42** (1376-1420), one of the oldest city halls in the Netherlands and a Gothic example for all its brothers and sisters that were built later, from Louvain to Audenarde and Brussels. Having admired its exterior, enter the impressive Gothic Hall and gaze in admiration at the polychrome floating ribs of the vaulted ceiling. Hiding on the right-hand side of this Gothic monument is the Basilica of the Holy Blood **01**. It was originally dedicated to both Our Lady and Saint Basil, and was built as a fortress church on

two levels between 1139 and 1157. The lower church has retained its Romanesque character. The upper chapel, which was originally little more than a kind of balcony, was gradually extended over the years to become a church in its own right. It was only during the 19th century that it was renovated in the neo-Gothic style that can be seen today. The sacred relic of the Holy Blood has been kept here since the 13th century. In a tradition dating back to at least 1304, each year on Ascension Day the relic is carried in the Holy Blood Procession, a popular event that captures the imagination of the entire city. Facing the basilica is the gleaming Renaissance façade of the old Civil Registry **03** (1534-1537, which now houses the City Archive **07** adjacent to the Liberty of Bruges **13**. Its showpiece is a splendid oak mantelpiece with an alabaster frieze (1529). From the adjoining Palace of the Liberty of Bruges (the front part of which dates from 1722), the countryside in a wide area around the city was once governed. After 1795, the building became a courtroom and since 1988 it has housed vari-

ous branches of the city administration. Once upon a time, Saint Donatian's Cathedral graced the spot directly in front of the City Hall. The church was torn down in 1799. The adjacent Deanery **17** (1655-1666), which still stands, was once the seat of the dean or spiritual leader of Saint Donation's. For those who are interested: it is still possible to see parts of the old cathedral in the cellar of the Crown Plaza Hotel.

Fishy stories

Proceed to Blinde-Ezelstraat, the little street to the left of the City Hall. Don't forget to look back at the lovely arch between the City Hall and the Old Civil Registry **03** **07**. Do you see Solomon? Left of him is the statue of Prosperity, to the right the statue of Peace.

According to tradition, Blinde-Ezelstraat (Blind Donkey Street) owes its name to a tavern of the same name. In olden days, the breweries that delivered beer to the taverns in the city used donkeys to turn their treadmills. To stop the poor beasts from realizing that they were just going around in circles, they were fitted with a blindfold. From the bridge, a few metres further along on the left, you can see the Meebrug (1390), one of the oldest bridges in the city.

Vismarkt **22** opens up immediately past the bridge.

Originally, fish was sold on the corner of the main market square, where the Historium **27** now stands, but the fish sellers were forced to move here in the

18th century because of the smell. In the covered arcade, specially erected for the purpose in 1821, fresh seafood was sold, a delicacy that only the rich could afford. Today you can still buy your fresh saltwater fish here every morning from Wednesday to Saturday. In the summer, the Vismarkt is a fun spot for regular dance and music events, where you can also get a bite to eat and something to drink.

Retrace your steps and turn left in front of the bridge towards Huidenvettersplein.

Whereas Vismarkt served the rich, Huidenvettersplein (Tanners Square) served the poor. No sea fish on the menu

Rozenhoedkaai

here, but affordable freshwater fish. The post in the middle of the square used to have a twin brother: between the two posts hung the scales that the fish were weighed on. The large, striking building dominating the square used to be the meeting hall of the tanners. Here they sold the cow hides that they had turned into leather. The location was not chosen by chance: tanning leather was a smelly business and because the wind mainly came from the north or north-west, the foul smells were blown away from the city, towards fields that were then unoccupied. So the statue on the corner of the building has good reason to turn his nose up...

Continue to Rozenhoedkaai. Keep right.

Rozenhoedkaai is the most photographed spot in Bruges. So, take out your camera! This was once the place where the salt traders loaded and unloaded their goods. Salt was the gold of the Middle Ages: you could use it both to preserve food and to give added flavour to your cooking. Its value is underlined by the fact that the origin of the modern word *salary* comes from the Latin word *sal*, which means 'salt'. Roman soldiers used to be paid in salt.

From Groeninge to the Bonifacius Bridge

Continue along Dijver.

In the middle of the 11th century, Everelmus went to live as a hermit in the oak wood along the Dijver. Along this atmospheric stretch of water, you will first find the College of Europe (numbers 9 to 11) **02**, an international postgraduate institution that focuses on European affairs, and then the Groeninge Museum (number 12) **25**, Bruges' most renowned museum. On display are world-famous masterpieces by Jan van Eyck, Hans Memling, Hugo van der Goes, Gerard David and many other Flemish primitives. The museum also has a valuable collection of Flemish expressionists, neoclassical top notch paintings from the 18th and 19th centuries and post-war modern art. Overall, the museum shows a complete overview of Belgian and southern Dutch painting from the 15th to the 20th century. The museum entrance is reached through a few picturesque courtyard gardens.

Would you like to find out more about the Flemish primitives? Then leaf through to the interview on pages 112-115 with Till-Holger Borchert, the Groeninge Museum's chief curator.

Continue along Dijver. The entrance gate to the Gruuthuse Museum 26 is on your left, just beyond the little bridge. This museum is closed for restoration until spring 2019 (subject to amendment).

Continue to Guido Gezelleplein, then turn left in front of the Church of Our Lady 15 33 and follow the narrow footpath to the picturesque Bonifacius Bridge. Due to renovation works, it is possible that the footpath will be closed for a time. If this is the case, follow the

🏠 ALMSHOUSES, THE QUICKEST WAY TO HEAVEN

These charitable dwellings were built from the 14th century onwards. Sometimes by the trade guilds, who wanted to offer their ageing members a roof over their heads; sometimes by widows or wealthy citizens, who hoped to secure their place in heaven with a display of

Christian charity. To stake their claim, each residential centre had its own chapel, where the residents offered prayers of thanks to God, as the household rules prescribed. Practically all of the almshouses have been carefully restored and modernised and offer cosy living to today's elderly, whilst their small yet picturesque gardens and white-painted façades offer welcoming peace and quiet to the present-day visitor. Feel free to enter these premises, but don't forget to respect their perfect tranquillity.

(On the City map the almshouses are indicated by 🏠 .)

The Four Horsemen of the Apocalypse

25

alternative route as indicated on the map (dotted line).

The crosses that you see all over the place don't belong to graves at all – they are crosses taken down from church steeples during the First World War to disorientate the enemy spies. The crosses have never been put up again. Close to the Bonifacius Bridge is Bruges' smallest Gothic window. Look up! It was through this window that the lords and ladies of Gruuthuse were able to peer down onto their private jetty. Across the bridge is the charming city garden Hof Arents of the Arentshuis (16th-19th century) **03**, an elegant 17th-century abode. The top floor houses work by the versatile British artist Frank Brangwyn. The ground floor is reserved for temporary exhibitions. The most striking features in the garden are the last two remaining columns of the Water Halls, the central storage depot for shipping that once stood on the Market Square, and the group of statues by Rik Poot (1924-2006), depicting *The Four Horsemen of the Apocalypse*: pestilence, war, famine and death. The religious theme of Rik Poots' statue group also

appealed centuries earlier to the artist Hans Memling, since the horsemen are also present in his *St. John Triptych*, which can be seen in the nearby St. John's Hospital **38**. The garden gate leads through to the Groeninge Museum **25**, where you can admire more works by Memling and his contemporaries.

On to the Beguinage!

Leave the garden once more through the narrow garden gate and turn left into Groeninge, a winding street. Turn right again at the intersection with Nieuwe Gentweg. Notice the Saint Joseph and the De Meulenaere alms-houses 🏠 (both from the 17th century). Continue down the street.

On the left-hand corner of Oude Gent-weg and Katelijnestraat is the Diamond Museum **19**, Bruges' most glittering museum and the place to be for all lovers of bling. It goes without saying that an inspiring diamond museum simply couldn't be absent in the most romantic city of the western hemisphere!

Turn left into Katelijnestraat, then immediately right into Wijngaardstraat.

Wijngaardplein

Cross Wijngaardplein – a stopping place for coachmen. A little further on, turn right onto the bridge beside the Sashuis (lock house) to enter the Beguinage. The bridge offers a fine view of the Minnewater.

The Minnewater used to be the landing stage of the barges or track boats that provided a regular connection between Bruges and Ghent. Today it is one of Bruges' most romantic beauty spots. Equally atmospheric, yet of a totally different nature, is the Beguinage. Although the 'Princely Beguinage Ten Wijngaarde' **02** **02**, founded in 1245, is no longer occupied by beguines (devout and celibate women who formed a religious community without taking holy orders), but by nuns of the Order of St. Benedict and a number of unmarried Bruges women, you can still form an excellent picture of what daily life looked like in the 17th century at the Beguine's house **04**. The imposing courtyard garden, the white painted house fronts and blessed peace create an atmosphere all of its own. The entrance gates are closed each day at 6.30 p.m. without fail.

Walk around the Beguinage and leave through the main gate. Turn left after the bridge and left again to reach Walplein.

De Halve Maan **10**, a brewery established as early as 1564, is at number 26 (on your left-hand side). This is Bruges' oldest active city brewery. Their speciality is *Brugse Zot* (Bruges' Fool), a spirited top-fermented beer made from malt, hop and special yeast. The name of the beer refers to the nickname of the Bruges townspeople, a name allegedly conferred upon them by Maximilian of Austria. In order to welcome the duke, the citizens paraded past him in a lavish procession of brightly coloured merrymakers and fools. When a short time later they asked their ruler to finance a new 'zothuis', or madhouse, his answer was as short as it was forceful: *'The only people I have seen here are fools. Bruges is one big madhouse. Just close the gates.'*

A splendid finish at Saint John's Hospital

Turn left into Zonnekemeers. Once across the water, enter the Oud Sint-Jan (Old St. John) site on the right. Feel

free to walk through the 19th century carriage house, if the gate is open.

The former St. John's Hospital (12th - 19th century) **38** which you can see in the right-hand corner, boasts a history stretching back more than 800 years. The oldest documents date from the year 1188! It was here that monks and nuns cared for pilgrims, travellers, the poor and the sick. Often, they came to the hospital to die. According to tradition, the painter Hans Memling was once a patient. After he was cured, he rewarded those who had treated him with four paintings. In the 19th century, two other Memling paintings found their way to the hospital, so that six of his masterpieces can now be admired here. Immediately in front of the convent of the old hospital stands the sculpture *The Veins of the Convent*, a work by the contemporary Italian artist Giuseppe Penone, which refers in a symbolic way to both the monastic way of life and the care function with which this site was once so closely associated. *Read more about Italian art in Bruges in the interview with Sonia Papili on pages 96-99.* Or how history still feeds the present – what could be more appropriate for a World Heritage City like Bruges!

Carriage house

Turn left at the corner and then go right immediately.

In the open space of the courtyard you will find the herb garden and the entrance to the 17th century pharmacy, which is well worth a visit. The herb garden contains all the necessary ingredients for 'gruut' or 'gruit', including lady's mantle, myrtle and laurel. You can find an explanation of what gruut is in *walk 2 on page 24*. Retrace your steps, turn left and walk through the passage. The entrance to the imposing medieval hospital wards, its church and chapel, the Diksmuide attic and the old dormitory are just around the corner to the right.

TIP

When you visit the Old St. John's Site, make sure you take a look at the 19th century infirmary wards. Some days, if you are lucky, you might catch a free concert by the Bruges harpist Luc Vanlaere. Moving and magical sounds that will make your visit to Bruges truly unforgettable. For more info, see www.harpmuziek.be

Walk 2
Bruges, a Burgundian city

Ceremonial tomb of Mary of Burgundy,
Church of Our Lady

When Philip the Bold, Duke of Burgundy, married Margaret of Dampierre, the daughter of the last Count of Flanders, in the 14th century, the county of Flanders suddenly found itself belonging to Burgundy. As the Burgundian court liked to stay in Bruges, the port city became a magnet for noblemen, merchants and artists. They naturally all wanted to get their share of the city's wealth. Today the Burgundian influence is still strongly felt throughout Bruges. Let's discover a northern city with a southern character.

WALK 2

» START

Guido Gezelleplein,
Church of Our Lady

» DISTANCE

2.5 km

» FINISH

Prinsenhof

• • • •
Alternative route

From Guido Gezelleplein to Markt

This square is named after the Flemish priest and poet Guido Gezelle (1830-1899). Take a seat on one of the square's benches and enjoy Gezelle's lovely statue and the side-view of the Church of Our Lady **15** **33**. Its one hundred and fifteen (and a half!)-metre high brick tower is sure proof of the craftsmanship of Bruges' artisans. The church is currently undergoing large-scale renovation work, so it is not possible to admire all its many fine works of art. However, Michelangelo's world-famous *Madonna and Child* can still be viewed. On your left is the striking residence of the lords of Gruuthuse, now the Gruuthuse Museum **26**. This, too, is undergoing renovation works and will be closed until spring 2019 (subject to amendment). The well (which unfortunately cannot be seen from the Guido Gezelleplein) and the tower were status symbols, and evidence of the Gruuthuse family's great wealth. They made their fortune from their exclusive rights to 'gruut', a herb mixture that, ages before hop, was used to flavour beer. Louis of Gruuthuse not only commanded the army of Charles the Bold, he was also the personal bodyguard to Mary of Burgundy. In addition, he was a patron of the arts and the owner of the famous Gruuthuse manuscript that bears his name, a famous medieval collection of no fewer than 147 songs (amongst other things). His family motto *'Plus est en vous'*

stands proudly above the door of the residence. Today, this translates as: 'There is more in you than you think'.

Continue along the narrow footpath to the left of the church. Due to renovation works, it is possible that this footpath will not be accessible.

Look up immediately beyond the bend. Do you see the chapel that seems to hold

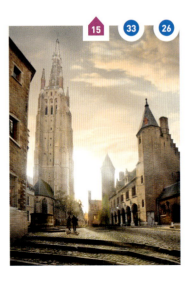

TIP

During the 16th century, the impressive mansion on the corner of the Wollestraat was once the home of Juan Perez de Malvenda, son of the Consul of the Spanish Nation and one of the city's most important residents. For a time, he kept the relic of the Holy Blood here. On the ground floor you can find a collection of all the things for which Belgium is famous: from a limitless choice of regional beers, through delicious biscuits and traditionally made jams, to fantastic old-fashioned sweets. The well-hidden terrace offers a magnificent view over the Rosary Quay.

the Gruuthuse Museum and the Church of Our Lady in a close embrace? As the lords of Gruuthuse were far too grand to mingle with the populace, they had their own private chapel high above the street, where they could follow Mass.

Retrace your steps, cross the attractive Gruuthuseplein and turn right into Dijver.

Number 12 is the Groeninge Museum **25** , Bruges' most famous museum. *An interview with chief curator Till-Holger Borchert is on pages 112-115.* Further along Dijver is one of the locations of the College of Europe **02** , numbers 9-11, an international postgraduate institution that focuses on Europe.

Carry on down Dijver and turn left into Wollestraat.

Perez de Malvenda **13** is an impressive mansion on the corner of Wollestraat. This building, originally a mansion dating from the 13th century, has been restored from top to bottom and now houses a food store. Just before the Markt are the Cloth Halls **09** , the Belfry's **05** warehouses and sales outlets.

There were numerous stables with all sorts of herbs for medicinal purpose and potions along the street side until long after the Burgundian period. Indeed, Bruges being an important trading centre could by then import and sell a variety of herbs from all over Europe.

Markt, Bruges' beating heart

Wollestraat leads to Markt.

The Market Square (Markt) is dominated by its Belfry **05** , for centuries the city's foremost edifice and the perfect lookout in case of war, fire or any other calamity. You can still climb to the top of the tower, but you will need to conquer no fewer than 366 steps to get there! Fortunately, there are a couple of places during your ascent where you can stop for a breather. Once at the top, you will be rewarded with an unforgettable panoramic view. At the foot of the Belfry are the world's most famous chippies ('frietkoten')! Roughly in the middle of the square stand the statues of Jan Breydel and Pieter de Coninck, two Bruges heroes, who since the publication of the historical novel *De Leeuw van Vlaanderen*

THE RIGHT TIME

On the Markt, at the very top of the late-Gothic corner house 'Bouchoute', which is currently home to the Meridian 3 tearoom, there is a shining ball decorated with gold leaf. At the time of the inauguration of the Brussels-Ghent-Bruges railway line, people were aware that the clocks in Belgium did not all keep the same time. This problem was solved in Bruges in 1837 by Professor Quetelet, who 'drew' a meridian on the ground and set up a noonday 'hand' that would show incontestably when it was twelve o'clock.

Markt

This meridian ran diagonally over the Markt and is now marked by a series of copper nails. When the shadow of the golden ball falls on the meridian, it is midday precisely: 12.00 p.m. local solar time.

(The Lion of Flanders) in the 19th century have enjoyed great popular acclaim because of their role in the Battle of the Golden Spurs (Flemish resistance against French rule). Their statue neatly looks out onto the Gothic revival style Provincial Court (Markt 3) **17**. Until the end of the 18th century, this side of the Markt was dominated by the Water Halls (Waterhalle), a large covered area where ships moored to be loaded and unloaded, right in the very

TIP

As you are climbing your way to the top of the Belfry tower, why not stop for a break at the vaulted treasure chamber, where the city's charters, seal and public funds were all kept during medieval times. You can make a second stop at the 'Stenen Vloer' (Stone Floor): here you will learn everything you ever wanted to know about the clock, the drum and the carillon of 47 harmonious bells, which together weigh a staggering 27 tons of pure bronze. With a little bit of luck

you will be able to see the bell-ringer right at the very top, playing the keyboard with his fist, just a few steps below the bells themselves.

heart of the city. In medieval times, the canals ran through and across the square, as indeed they still do, although they are now in underground tunnels. Do you feel like taking a relaxing break from all that walking? Then why not treat yourself to a coach ride and explore the city for half an hour from the luxury of a horse-drawn carriage *[see page 47]* or for 30 minutes from the back of a man-powered bike carriage *[see page 50]*. If neither of these is really your thing, you can always take the classic 50-minute City Tour by minibus *[see page 48]*. Afterwards, you can simply resume your walk where you left off.

From Markt to Jan van Eyckplein

Keep Markt on your left and continue straight ahead to Vlamingstraat.
Since the 13th century, this used to be the harbour area's shopping street. A fair number of banks had a branch here, and wine taverns were two a penny. Each of these had (and still has) a deep cellar where French and Rhenish wines could easily be stacked. In the medieval vaulted cellars of Taverne Curiosa (Vlamingstraat 22), the alcohol-laden atmosphere of those bygone days can still be inhaled. Halfway along Vlamingstraat is the elegant City Theatre **43** on your left. This royal theatre (1869) is one of Europe's best-preserved city theatres. Behind the Neo-Renaissance façade lie a magnificent auditorium and a palatial foyer.

TIP

Since as long ago as 1897, two green painted mobile chippies have stood in front of the Belfry. It is definitely the best place in town to buy – and sell – chips, good for the annual consumption of several tons of fast food! The stalls are open nearly every hour of the day and night, so that you never need to go hungry!

Papageno, the bird seller from Mozart's opera, *The Magic Flute*, guards the entrance. His score lies scattered on the square opposite.

Continue along Vlamingstraat and turn right into Kortewinkel just before the water.
Somewhat hidden from gazing eyes, Kortewinkel boasts a unique 16th-century wooden house front. It is one of only two left in the city (you will come across

Vlamingstraat

SWANS ON THE CANALS

After the death of Mary of Burgundy (1482), Bruges went through some troubled times. The townspeople, enraged by new taxes Maximilian of Austria, Mary's successor, had imposed upon them, rose in revolt against their new ruler. As Maximilian was locked up in House Craenenburg on the Market Square, he helplessly witnessed the torture and eventual beheading of his bailiff and trusted councillor Pieter Lanchals (Long Neck). A stubborn old legend says that when the duke came back to power, he took his vengeance on the local people by forcing them to keep 'long necks' or swans on the canals for all time. In reality, however, swans have been swimming on the canals since the beginning of the 15th century, when they were seen as a status symbol of the city's power and wealth.

the other one further along this walk). Just a few metres on is another exciting discovery at number 10. The former Jesuit House **09** has a magnificent hidden courtyard garden. Is its door open? Then walk in and enjoy its heavenly peace.

Kortewinkel turns into Spaanse Loskaai, the home port of the Spanish merchants until the end of the 16th century.

At 700 years of age, the picturesque bridge you pass on the left, the Augustijnenbrug (Augustinians' Bridge), is one of the oldest in Bruges. The stone seats were originally intended to display the wares of the diligent sellers. The bridge affords an excellent view of the house in the right-hand corner, which connects Spanjaardstraat with Kortewinkel. This was once House De Noodt Gods but is also said to be a haunted house, according to the locals. When an amorous monk was rejected by a nun, the man murdered her and then committed suicide. Ever since they have been haunting that ramshackle building...

Continue along Spaanse Loskaai, go down the first street on your right and proceed to Oosterlingenplein.

During Bruges' golden century, this was the fixed abode of the so-called 'Oosterlingen' (Easteners) or German merchants. Their imposing warehouse took up the entire left corner of the square. Today the only remnant is the building to the right of Hotel Bryghia. Their warehouse must have been truly grand!

Beyond Oosterlingenplein is Woensdagmarkt, the square on which the statue of the painter Hans Memling attracts all attention. Turn right into Genthof.

Here the second of two authentic medieval wooden house fronts draws attention. Notice that each floor juts out a little more than the previous one. This building technique, which helped to avoid water damage (but also created extra space), was consequently used in various architectural styles.

Burgundian Manhattan

Proceed to Jan van Eyckplein.

This was the Manhattan of Burgundian Bruges, the place where everything happened. It was here that ships moored, were loaded and unload, and paid their tolls. In this unremitting hustle and bustle, a cacophony of languages was heard above the din, one sounding even louder than the other. What a soundtrack! Each business transaction required a few local sounds too, of course, as there always had to be a Bruges broker present who would naturally pocket his cut. On the corner, the 16th-century House De Rode Steen (number 8) has been sparkling in all its glory since its restoration (the first building in Bruges to be renovated thanks to a subsidy from the city) in 1877. At numbers 1-2 is the Old Tollhouse (1477) **05** **21**, where the tolls levied on the goods and products of both regional and international trade were collected. On the left-hand side of this truly monumental building stands the Rijkepijnders House, the smallest

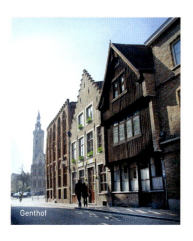
Genthof

TIP

The Genthof has in recent years attracted a variety of different arts and crafts. There is a glass-blower, a trendy vintage store and a number of contemporary art galleries. And on the corner you can find 't Terrastje, the café with probably the smallest terrace in Bruges.

05

house in Bruges. This was the meeting place of the *rijkepijnders*, the agents who supervised the porters and the dock-workers employed to load and unload the ships. People with sharp eyes may be able to spot some of these heavily-laden *pijnders* depicted on the facade.

Continue along Academiestraat.
Right on the corner with Jan van Eyck-plein is another remarkable building, distinguished by its striking tower. This is the Burghers' Lodge (Poortersloge) 15 , a 15th-century building where the burgesses of the city (patricians and merchants) once used to meet. This building is normally not accessible to the public, but during the Bruges Trien-nial 2018 *(see page 76-77)* the Burghers' Lodge will serve as a central info-point and will therefore exceptionally be open for visitors.
In a wall niche, the Bruges Bear, an important city symbol, stands proud and upright. From 1720 to 1890, the Burghers' Lodge was the home of the Municipal Academy of Fine Arts, whose collection later formed the basis for the Groeninge Museum. From 1912 to 2012, the building served as the home of the State Archives.

Do you want to know more about the Bruges Triennial 2018? Turn to page 104-107, where you can read an interview with the co-curator, Michel Dewilde.

Proceed to Grauwwerkersstraat.
The little square connecting Acade-miestraat with Grauwwerkersstraat has been known as 'Beursplein' since time immemorial.
Here merchants were engaged in high-quality trade. The merchant houses of Genoa (Genuese Lodge, later renamed 'Saaihalle' 08 and today Belgian Fries Museum (Frietmuseum 22), Florence

THE LITTLE BEAR OF BRUGES

When Baldwin Iron Arm, the first Count of Flanders, visited Bruges for the first time, the first creature he saw was a huge, snow-covered brown bear. According to the legend, all this happened in the 9th century. After a fierce fight, the count succeeded in killing the animal. In homage to the courageous beast, he proclaimed the bear to be the city's very own symbol. Today 'Bruges' oldest inhabitant' in the niche of the Burghers' Lodge is festively rigged out during exceptional celebrations. The Bruges Bear is holding the coat of arms of the Noble Company of the White Bear, a chivalric order of knights famed for their jousting tournaments, which was founded shortly after Baldwin I had beaten the 'white' bear and which held its meetings in the Burghers' Lodge.

(now De Florentijnen restaurant) and Venice (now pool bar The Monk) once stood here side by side like brothers. In front of house Ter Beurse (1276) **11**, the central inn, merchants from all over Europe used to gather to arrange business appointments and conduct exchange transactions. The Dutch word for stock exchange became 'beurs',

derived from the name of the house. Many other languages would take over this term, such as French (bourse) or Italian (borsa).

Turn into Grauwwerkersstraat and stop immediately in your tracks.
The side wall of house Ter Beurse **11**, and more precisely the part between the two sets of ground-floor windows, bears the signatures of the stonecutters. This way, everybody knew which mason cut which stones and how much each mason had to be paid. The house next-door to house Ter Beurse, called 'de Kleine Beurse' (the Little Stock Exchange), still sits on its original street level.

Turn left into Naaldenstraat.
On your right, Bladelin Court **09** with its attractive tower looms up ahead. Pieter Bladelin, portrayed above the gate whilst praying to the Virgin Mary,

PRINSENHOF GOSSIP

> As Philip the Good hadn't yet laid eyes on his future wife (Isabella of Portugal), he sent Jan van Eyck to Portugal to paint her portrait. This way the duke wanted to make certain he had made the right choice. The duke's ploy worked, because history teaches us that the couple had a happy marriage.

> Although the popular Mary of Burgundy incurred only seemingly minor injuries as a result of a fall with her horse, the accident would eventually lead to her death from a punctured lung at Prinsenhof. Back in those times there was no cure for inflammation.

> During the hotel renovation, no fewer than 578 silver coins, minted between 1755 and 1787, were dug up. After some careful counting and calculations, it is assumed that the energetic English nuns, who lived there at that time, entrusted the coins to the soil so as to prevent the advancing French troops from stealing their hard-earned capital.

first rented out and then sold his mansion to the Florentine banking family, the Medici, who ran a branch of their bank here in the 15th century. Today, this property is owned by the Catholic University of Leuven and the Sisters of Our Lady of the Seven Sorrows.

Somewhat further along, next to another ornamental tower, turn right into Boterhuis, a winding cobbled alley that catapults you back straight into the Middle Ages. Keep right, pass Saint James's Church and turn left into Moerstraat.

The Dukes of Burgundy and the vast majority of foreign merchants patronised Saint James's Church **22**. Their extravagant gifts have left their glittering mark on the interior.

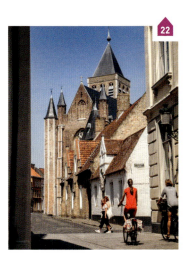

Prinsenhof (the Princes' Court), home base of the Dukes of Burgundy

Turn left into Geerwijnstraat and carry on to Muntplein.

Muntplein (Coin Square) belonged to nearby Prinsenhof **16**. As you might have guessed, this was where Bruges' mint was situated. The statue *Flandria Nostra* (Our Flanders), which represents a noblewoman on horseback, was designed by the Belgian sculptor Jules Lagae (1862-1931).

At the end of Geerwijnstraat turn right into Geldmuntstraat. The walk's finishing point is Prinsenhof.

We end the walk on a highlight. Prinsenhof used to be the palace of the Flemish counts and Burgundy dukes. This impressive mansion, originally seven times the size of what you see today, was expanded in the 15th century by Philip the Good to celebrate his (third) marriage to Isabella of Portugal. When Charles the Bold remarried Margaret of York, the largest bathhouse in Europe, a game court (to play 'jeu de paume' or the palm game, the forerunner of tennis) and a zoological garden were all added to the ducal residence. It is no surprise that Prinsenhof not only became the favourite pied-à-terre of the Dukes of Burgundy, but also the nerve centre of their political, economic and cultural ambitions. Both Philip the Good (d.1467) and Mary of Burgundy (d.1482) breathed their last here. After the death of the popular Mary of Burgundy, the palace's fortunes declined, until it eventually ended up in private hands. In the 17th century, English nuns converted it into a boarding school for girls of well-to-do parents. Nowadays, you can stay in the Prinsenhof Castle in true princely style.

TIP

Whoever wants to get a really good impression of the magnificence of this city castle and its elegant gardens should follow the signs in the Ontvangersstraat to the hotel car park at Moerstraat 46. Of course, you can always treat yourself – and your nearest and dearest – to a princely drink in the bar of the hotel: the perfect way to enjoy the grandeur and luxury of the complex.

Walk 3
Strolling through silent Bruges

Ramparts

Although the parishes of Saint Anne and Saint Giles are known as places of great tranquillity, the fact that they are off the beaten track does not mean that the visitor will be short of adventure. How about a row of nostalgic windmills? Or perhaps some unpretentious working-class neighbourhoods, or a couple of exclusive gentlemen's clubs? Will you be able to take in all these impressions? Don't worry. After the tour we invite you to catch your breath in Bruges' oldest cafe!

DAMPOORT

35

WALK 3

» START
Choco-Story
(Wijnzakstraat 2)

» DISTANCE
4 km

» FINISH
Café Vlissinghe
(Blekersstraat 2)

START

FINISH

MARKT

BURG

Koningsbrug

From Choco-Story to Gouden-Handstraat

Choco-Story (Chocolate Museum) **14** is the perfect starting point for the longest walk in this guide. This museum not only dips you in the yummy history of chocolate and cocoa, it also offers extensive chocolate tasting. If you wish, you can also buy your supplies here. No doubt the chocolate will help you to keep up a brisk pace! At the same address, Lumina Domestica **31** contains the world's largest collection of lamps and lights. The museum also houses six thousand antiques.

Turn left into Sint-Jansstraat, carry on to Korte Riddersstraat and continue until the end of the street.
Saint Walburga's Church **24** rises up in all its magnificence right in front of you. This Baroque edifice (1619-1642) boasts a remarkable marble communion rail and high altar. Nearby, at number 5 there is a splendid 18th-century mansion.

Continue down Koningstraat to the bridge.

This bridge, which connects poetic Spinolarei with Spiegelrei, affords a lovely view of Oud Huis Amsterdam on your left. Today this historic town house (Spiegelrei 3) is an elegant hotel. This part of the city used to be mainly populated by the English and Scots. The English merchants even had their own 'steegere', or stair where their goods were unloaded. The stair is still there, and the street connecting it is appropriately called Engelsestraat. The dignified white school building (number 15) across the bridge was once a college of English Jesuits.

Saint Giles', home base of workmen and artists

Cross the bridge, turn right along Spiegelrei and turn into Gouden-Handstraat, the fourth street on your left.
In the 15th century, Gouden-Handstraat and the parish of Saint Giles were known as the artists' quarter. Hans Memling may have lived a few streets further down in Sint-Jorisstraat; the fact of the matter is that Jan van Eyck had a studio in Gouden-Handstraat,

and that his somewhat lesser-known fellow artists also used to congregate in this neighbourhood.

Turn right into Sint-Gilliskerkstraat.

This street bumps into Saint Giles' Church **20** in the heart of the tranquil quarter of Saint Giles'. Initially a chapel, this building was upgraded to a parish church in 1258. In spite of its interior in Gothic revival style and its superb paintings, the church takes on the appearance of a simple, sturdy village church. Don't be misled. In and around the church countless famous painters were buried, such as Hans Memling (d.1494), in his time the best-paid painter, Lanceloot Blondeel (d.1561) and Pieter Pourbus (d.1584). Their graves and the cemetery may have disappeared, but their artists' souls still hover in the air.

Walk around the church and turn into Sint-Gilliskoorstraat.

Although the workmen's dwellings in these streets are rather small, they nevertheless display a bricked-up window. As it happened, a tax on windows was levied in 1800. As a consequence, a large number of windows were walled up.

From Potterierei to the 'vesten' (ramparts)

Turn left into Langerei at the end of the street. Cross the lovely Snaggaardbrug, the first bridge you get to, into Potterierei. Turn left and follow the canal for some time.

After a fair distance along Potterierei is Bruges' Major Seminary (number 72) **05** on your right. A unique place with a lush orchard and meadows with cows at pasture. Between 1628 and 1642, a new Cistercian Abbey (the Dune Abbey)

Woensdagmarkt

BRUGES AND THE SEA

For centuries, Langerei ensured the city's wealth. This canal ran to Damme, where it was connected to a large lock, called 'Speie', which in turn was connected to the Zwin, a deep sea channel and tidal inlet. While Damme developed into an outport, Bruges grew into

Northwestern Europe's greatest business centre of the Middle Ages. The arts flourished, culture thrived, prosperity seemed to be set for all eternity. The tide turned when Mary of Burgundy suddenly passed away in 1482. The relations between Bruges and the Burgundians turned sour and the Burgundian court left the city. The foreign merchants and their wealth followed in its wake. The Zwin continued to silt up and Bruges lost her privileged commercial position. As a result, and compounded by a series of political intrigues, the city fell into a deep winter sleep.

was erected here, which later on would achieve great fame for the wealth and erudition of its occupants. During the French Revolution, the abbey was brought under public ownership, and the abbot and monks were chased away. The 17th-century abbey buildings were first used as a military hospital and then as a military depot and a grammar school before they were eventually taken over by the Major Seminary in 1833. Up to the present day, the Seminary has been training Catholic priests here. Nowadays, there is also a research and training centre for the University of the United Nations 10 . Just a few yards further down at number 79B is Our Lady of the Pottery 16 34 . Its history goes back to the 13th century. Diligent nuns used to treat pilgrims, travellers and the sick here. From the 15th century onwards, it be-

came a home for the care of the elderly. The Gothic church with its Baroque interior and its rich collection of works of art, accumulated by the hospital

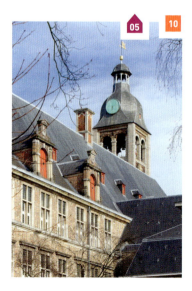

throughout the centuries, is a hidden gem that is certainly well worth a visit!

Carry on to the lock and spend some time by the water.

This idyllic spot is where the canal Damse Vaart heads out across the other side of the ring road towards the equally romantic town of Damme. It's hard to believe that this area around the canal was once a scene of great controversy. Up until the Eighty Years' War, Bruges was connected to the Dutch town of Sluis by way of Damme. Ambitious Napoleon Bonaparte had the connection to the tidal inlet of the Zwin, the natural predecessor of the Damse Vaart, dredged by Spanish prisoners of war so as to create a watercourse that would run all the way to Antwerp. His plan then was to develop the port city of Antwerp into a naval base, which would enable him to avoid the English sea blockade. Napoleon's project left Damme cut in twain. The wild plans of the little general were never carried out in full, and by 1814

TIP

Have we sparked your curiosity? Or do you just like to do things the easy way? If so, leave your bike and car at home and jump aboard for a voyage on the Lamme Goedzak 🚢 the most stylish way to reach the town of Damme. Step back in time during this nostalgic journey.

(For more information see page 51)

Napoleon's role in Flanders had come to an end. Under the impulse of William I, King of the Netherlands, who also saw the value of a connecting canal, the digging work continued until 1824. Belgian independence (1830) meant that the project was finally terminated, by which time it had reached as far as Sluis. Today the low traffic bicycle path skirting the canal is a most attractive route linking Bruges with Damme. The trip is highly recommended, as it traverses *le plat pays*, that flat country made famous by Jacques Brel. Imagine! In the middle of a unique pol-

Sasplein

THE ARCHERS' GUILD: 120 MEN AND 2 QUEENS!

Two centuries-old archery clubs are now to be found in what was one of the poorer districts of Bruges in the 19th century. High and dry on the same hill as the Sint-Janshuis Mill, at the bottom left, stands the Sint-Joris (St. George's) Guild **40**, a crossbow guild that specializes in two archery disciplines: shooting at targets on the ground and shooting at feathered discs in a tower. To the right, with its eye-catching target tower, is the home of the Sint-Sebastiaan (St. Sebastian) Guild **41**, a longbow society. This guild goes back more than six centuries, which makes it unique in the world. The society numbers about 120 male members and two notable female honorary members: the Belgian queen Mathilde and the British queen. Ever since the exiled English king Charles II took up residence in Bruges in the 17th century, the city and the British Royal Family have always been closely associated. Within the St. Sebastian Archery Guild, Charles founded both the British Grenadier Guards and the Life Guards Regiment.

der landscape this truly poetic canal strip, bordered by lofty poplars bended down by eternal westerly winds.

Turn right and carry on along the Vesten (ramparts), which surround the city like a ring of green.

In the 16th century, more than thirty windmills were turning their sails here. Today only four are left. In the 18th century, the millers stood by helplessly when bread consumption took a dive and people started to consume more potatoes. Eventually steam machines would take over the millers' tasks. One of the mills, the Sint-Janshuis Mill **39**, can still be visited today. A miller will be happy not only to give you an explana-

tion of his craft, but will also show you how the milling is done. It is well worth climbing the slopes on which the Sint-Janshuis Mill and the Bonne Chiere Mill (near the Kruispoort/Cross Gate **12**) proudly stand. From the top of these mill mounds, there is a fantastic panoramic view across the city. This is the perfect spot to brush up on your amassed knowledge of Bruges. And there's more! Down below on your right is the Verloren Hoek (the Lost Corner), now an authentic working-class district, but back in the 19th century an impoverished neighbourhood with such a bad reputation that even the police didn't dare enter its streets.

Silent Bruges

Descend down the slope and turn right into Rolweg.

Right on the corner is the Gezelle Museum **24**, the birthplace of Guido Gezelle (1830-1899), one of Flanders' most venerable poets. On display are handwritten letters, writing material and a deliciously peaceful garden with an age-old Corsican pine. Gezelle's parents worked here as gardener and caretaker, in exchange for which they and their family received free board and lodging. Little Guido grew up in these idyllic surroundings. He would eventually return to Bruges many years later and after many a peregrination. Upon his return, he became curate of Saint Walburga's Church **24**. He also took over the running of the English Convent **04**, where he would die. These were his last words, reportedly: *'I have so loved hearing the birds singing.'* Here, in this most verdant part of Bruges, we still know precisely what the priest and poet meant.

Turn into Balstraat, the second street on the left.

This picturesque working-man's alley houses the Museum of Folk Life (Volkskundemuseum) **44**. The 17th-century row of single-room dwellings, restored and converted into authentic artisans' interiors such as a milliner's, a confectioner's and a small classroom, will

TIP

Interested in a little something 'extra'? Then go and take a look at the Albrecht Rodenbachstraat, another of the city's hidden gems. This green suburb avant la lettre offers an almost unbroken succession of stepgables and other fascinating facades, each fronted by a delightful little garden.

take you back to bygone days. The tower of the 15th-century Jerusalem Chapel **08** can easily be spotted from these premises. This chapel was commissioned by the Adornes, a prominent Bruges merchant family of Genovese origin, who lived in a magnificent mansion **01** on the Peperstraat. In 1470, Anselm Adornes collected one of his sons (the father had no fewer than six-teen children) in Padua to set off on a pilgrimage to the Holy Land. Upon his return to Bruges, Anselm decided to build an exact copy of the Church of the Holy Sepulchre. The result was remarkable. In the adjacent Adornes Estate **01**, you will make closer acquaintance with this prominent family and its intriguing history.

Café Vlissinghe

At the crossroads, turn right into Jeruzalemstraat; then, at the church, left onto Sint-Annaplein.

The tiny square is dominated by the apparently simple Church of Saint Anne **19**. Its exterior may be austere, but its interior is one of Bruges' most splendid examples of Baroque architecture. As this neighbourhood gradually became more prestigious, the church did the same!

With the church behind you, follow the Sint-Annakerkstraat and then turn right into Sint-Annarei.

At the corner of the confluence of the two waterways, one of Bruges' most handsome town houses is proudly showing off its Rococo credentials (Sint-Annarei no. 22). Sit yourself down on a bench in the shadow and enjoy this exceptional view.

Retrace your steps for just a few yards and turn left into Blekersstraat next to the bridge.

Café Vlissinghe at number 2 is undoubtedly Bruges' oldest café. This has been a tavern since 1515. It is no surprise then that you will find oodles of ambiance here. It is therefore the perfect place to settle down and let the wonderful memories of your walk slowly sink in. A local beer will be your ideal companion. Cheers!

Rozenhoedkaai

Know your way around **Bruges**

Exploring Bruges

The canals of Bruges

You might want to stroll, amble and saunter down the streets of Bruges all day long. However, why not try to see the city from a different perspective? During a walking or bicycle tour, a guide will show you numerous secret places. Maybe you would prefer a boat trip on the mysterious canals – an unforgettable experience! And a ride in a horse-drawn carriage must surely be the perfect romantic outing. Sport-lovers can even do a guided run around the city. Or perhaps you simply want to tour all the highlights as quickly and as comfortably as possible? That's exactly what the minibuses do, and along the route you get plenty of explanation as well. Or what about a flight in a hot-air balloon, a ride in a bike carriage or a modern exploration on a segway? The choice is yours!

MYSTERIOUS CANALS AND THE RHYTHMIC CLOPPING OF HOOVES: TWO EXCURSIONS YOU DON'T WANT TO MISS

The canals of Bruges - the 'reien' - are the arteries of the city. Nothing is as pleasant as chugging along in a boat on a sunny day as you sail past all the most beautiful places in the city. From the 'reien', it's almost like you are seeing Bruges for the first time. Unexpected views, hidden romantic corners, secret gardens: you discover them all from your vantage point on the water. There are regular daily sailings from any of the five moorings in the heart of the city. A voyage lasts half an hour and takes you past all the most photogenic spots Bruges has to offer.

Or why not opt for a romantic coach ride through the winding streets, over centuries old squares and charming bridges of the historic city centre? For half an hour, you can sit back and enjoy the rhythmic clopping of horse's hooves as you take in all the most picturesque spots in Bruges. During your ride the coachman will give you an expert commentary and about half way you make a short stop at the Beguinage.

Bruges by boat

OPEN > Sailings guaranteed from March to mid-November: in principle, daily, 10.00 a.m.-6.00 p.m., last sailing at 5.30 p.m.
PRICE > €8; children aged 4 to 11 (accompanied by an adult): €4; children under 4: free

Bruges by horse-drawn carriage

OPEN > Daily, 9.00 a.m. to at least 6.00 p.m., but no later than 10.00 p.m.
PRICE PER CARRIAGE > €50; max. 5 people
MEETING POINT > Markt, but at the Burg square on Wednesday morning
INFO > www.hippo.be/koets

🚌 Bruges by bus

City Tour Bruges

The mini buses of City Tour provide a guided tour that will take you past all the most beautiful places in Bruges. Every half hour, they depart for a 50 minute drive along the most important highlights of the town.

OPEN > Daily, every half hour (also on public holidays). The first bus leaves at 10.00 a.m. During the period 1/11 to 31/1 the last bus leaves at 4.00 p.m.; 1/2 to 9/2 at 4.30 p.m.; 10/2 to 28/2 at 5.00 p.m.; 1/3 to 15/3 and 16/10 to 31/10 at 5.30 p.m.; 16/3 to 30/4 and 1/10 to 15/10 at 6.00 p.m. and 1/5 to 30/9 at 7.00 p.m. There are no departures at 6.30 p.m.

ADDITIONAL CLOSING DATE > 17/9
PRICE > Including headphones with explanation (available in 16 languages): €20; children aged 6 to 11 years: €15; children under 6: free
MEETING POINT > Markt
INFO > Tel. +32 (0)50 35 50 24 (Monday to Friday, 10.00 a.m.-12.00 p.m.), www.citytour.be

Photo Tour Brugge

Whether you are a photography expert or a novice, during the Photo Tour Andy McSweeney takes you to all the most photogenic spots in the city.

OPEN > Daily: *Edges of Brugge* (10.00 a.m.-12.00 p.m.) focuses on the side streets and canals; *Essential Brugge* (1.00 p.m.-3.00 p.m.) zooms in on the top sights; during *Hidden Brugge* (4.00 p.m.-6.00 p.m.) you will go in search of some of the city's less well-known corners; the private tour *Shades of Brugge* (8.00 p.m.-11.00 p.m.) allows you to experience the evening delights of the city.

PRICE > €60 (max. 5 photographers per tour); private tour: €220 (max. 3 photographers); children younger than 4 years: free; each participating photographer can bring along a non-photographer free of charge. Prior reservation is necessary, but is possible on the day.
MEETING POINT > Basilica of the Holy Blood, on the Burg square
LANGUAGES > English, but on request also Dutch and/or French
INFO > Tel. +32 (0)486 17 52 75, www.phototourbrugge.com

Bruges by heart

Top-quality walk with local guides

During this exclusive walk (max. 16 people), a city guide will take you on a fascinating journey. Not only will you discover many of the great historic buildings and sites, but also some hidden gems and secret places. The walk starts with a breathtaking view of the city from the roof terrace of the Concert Hall. A unique experience!

OPEN > Find out via www.visitbruges.be when you can book a place on one of the walks or pop into one of the  info offices.

PRICE > (Subject to amendment) €12.50; children younger than 12 years: free

MEETING POINT > The walk starts from the info office  't Zand (Concert Hall)

LANGUAGES > English, Dutch, French. During certain periods, also in German and Spanish.

TICKETS > Info offices  Markt (Historium) and 't Zand (Concert Hall) or via www.ticketsbrugge.be

APP > Another way to explore the city on foot (or by bike) is to use the free Xplore Bruges app. *You can find more info on www.xplorebruges.be on page 98.*

INFO > Tel. +32 (0)50 44 46 46, www.visitbruges.be

Running around Bruges

Tourist Run Brugge – guided tours

Accompanied by a guide you run – at a gentle pace – through the streets and alleyways of Bruges. The circuit, which ends on the Markt, is 9.5 km long. With the explanation that you receive along the way, you should allow 1 to 1.30 hours for completion.

OPEN > Daily, tours at 7.00 a.m., 8.00 a.m., 9.00 a.m., 5.00 p.m., 6.00 p.m., 7.00 p.m., 8.00 p.m. and 9.00 p.m. Reservation is required.

PRICE > €30/person; for 2 runners: €25/person; 3 runners or more: €20/person

MEETING POINT > At the statue of Jan Breydel and Pieter de Coninck on the Markt. If requested in advance, you can be picked up from wherever you are staying (hotel, etc.).

LANGUAGES > English, Dutch, French, German

INFO > Tel. +32 (0)473 88 37 17, www.touristrunbrugge.be

Bruges by bike

QuasiMundo Biketours: Bruges by bike

Riding through the narrow streets, you will discover the charming character of Bruges. The fascinating stories of the guide will catapult you back in time to the era when counts and dukes ruled over the city.

OPEN > 1/4 to 30/12: daily, 10.00 a.m.-12.30 p.m. Reservation is required.

PRICE > Including bike, raincoat and drink in a local bar: €30; youngsters aged 9 to 26: €28; children under 9: free. If you bring your own bike: €18 or €16 (youngsters aged 9 to 26)

MEETING POINT > At the City Hall

LANGUAGES > English, but also Dutch, French, German and Spanish on request

INFO > Tel. +32 (0)50 33 07 75 or +32 (0)478 28 15 21, www.quasimundo.eu

Also see 'Guided tours through Bruges' wood- and wetlands', page 142.

🚴 Fietskoetsen Brugge (Bike carriages)

Discover all the city's most romantic places and historical sites of interest in a unique and ecological way. A personal guide will take you on a bike carriage tour of 30 minutes.

OPEN > 8/1 to 28/2: on Saturday and Sunday, 11.00 a.m.-6.00 p.m.; 1/3 to 31/12: daily, 11.00 a.m.-6.00 p.m.

PRICE PER BIKE CARRIAGE > €24; max. 3 people. Reservations can be made through the website

MEETING POINT > On the Markt, outside the De Reyghere book store; but on the Burg square on Wednesday mornings

LANGUAGES > English, Dutch, French, German and Spanish

INFO > Tel. +32 (0)478 40 95 57, www.fietskoetsenbrugge.be

🚶 🛜 Bruges on a segway

Want to explore Bruges in an original manner? You can, with a segway: an electric, self-stabilizing two-wheeled vehicle that you steer from a standing position. You can follow the historic city tour, the chocolate tour, the brewery tour (with a visit to the Halve Maan brewery) or the evening tour with dinner.

OPEN > Monday: tours at 12.00 p.m., 2.00 p.m., 4.00 p.m. and 6.00 p.m.; Tuesday, Thursday and Friday: tours at 10.00 a.m., 12.00 p.m., 2.00 p.m., 4.00 p.m. and 6.00 p.m.; Saturday and Sunday: tours at 10.00 a.m., 12.00 p.m., 2.00 p.m. and 4.00 p.m.; Wednesday: by appointment only

PRICE > City tour: €40 (1 hour) or €55 (2 hours); other tours are more expensive. Prior reservation is necessary, but is possible on the day itself (min. 2 people).

LANGUAGES > English, Dutch, French and German

INFO AND RESERVATIONS > Oud Sint-Jan site (left of restaurant/lounge bar B-In), tel. +32 (0)50 68 87 70 or +32 (0)495 90 60 60, www.segwaybrugge.be

Bruges by hot air balloon

🛜 Bruges Ballooning

The most adventurous and probably the most romantic way to discover Bruges is by hot-air balloon. Bruges

Ballooning organizes both a morning flight and an evening flight over Bruges. The whole trip lasts for three hours, with at least one hour in the air.

OPEN > 1/4 to 31/10: daily flights, but only if booked in advance; bookings can be made on the day.

PRICE > €180; children aged 4 to 12: €110

MEETING POINT > You will be picked up and dropped off wherever you are staying.

LANGUAGES > English, Dutch, French, Spanish and Portuguese

INFO > Tel. +32 (0)475 97 28 87, www.bruges-ballooning.com

🚢 Lamme Goedzak (steam wheeler) Damme

The nostalgic river boat 'Lamme Goedzak', with room for 170 passengers, sails back and forth between Bruges and the centre of Damme.

OPEN > During Easter holiday and 1/5 to 14/10: departures from Bruges to Damme, daily at 12.00 p.m., 2.00 p.m., 4.00 p.m. and 6.00 p.m.; departures from Damme to Bruges, daily at 11.00 a.m., 1.00 p.m., 3.00 p.m. and 5.00 p.m.

PRICE > €8.50 (one-way ticket) or

€11.50 (return ticket); 65+: €8 (one-way ticket) or €10.50 (return ticket); children aged 3 to 11: €7 (one-way ticket) or €9.50 (return ticket)

MEETING POINT > Embark in Bruges at the Noorweegse Kaai 31 (City map: J1). Embarkation in Damme: Damse Vaart-Zuid

INFO > Tel. +32 (0)50 28 86 10, www.bootdamme-brugge.be

Port Cruise Zeebrugge

The 75-minute port cruise departs from the old fishing port. The tour takes in the naval base, the Pierre Vandamme Lock (one of the largest locks in the world), the gas terminal, the wind turbine park, the 'tern' island, the cruise ships and the dredging vessels. You will also see how the massive container ships are unloaded at the quay. A unique experience!

OPEN > 1/4 to 15/10: weekends and public holidays round trip at 2.00 p.m.; 1/7 to 31/8: daily round trip at 2.00 p.m. and 4.00 p.m; 1/8 to 15/8: daily extra round trip at 11.00 a.m.

PRICE > On board: €12.50; 60+: €11; children aged 3 to 11: €9. Tickets can also be purchased online at a reduced price.

MEETING POINT > Embark at the landing stage at the end of the Tijdokstraat (old fishing port), Zeebrugge

LANGUAGES > English, Dutch, French and German. You can also download the commentary on your smartphone (free).

INFO > Tel. +32 (0)59 70 62 94 (for extra departures outside the fixed sailing times), www.franlis.be

Museums, places of interest and attractions

Beguinage

Some places are so special, so breathtaking or so unique that you simply have to see them. Bruges is filled to the brim with wonderful witnesses of a prosperous past. Although the Flemish primitives are undoubtedly Bruges' showpiece attraction, museum devotees in search of much more will not be disappointed. Indeed, the Bruges range of attractions is truly magnificent. From modern plastic art by way of Michelangelo's world-famous *Madonna and Child* to the Lace Centre. It's all there for you to discover!

CONCERTGEBOUW CIRCUIT - A NEW LOOK AT BRUGES CLASSICAL MUSIC CITY

First and foremost, Bruges impresses with its 'classics' in stone and its romantic city views, but did you know that the city also has an outstanding reputation for classical music? This reputation dates back to medieval times, when the world-renowned Flemish polyphonists brightened up the city palaces of the rich Burgundians with their delightful melodies. Nowadays, Bruges continues to be an all-year-round home for concerts and festivals of world-class classical music. In the imposing Concert Hall, with its celebrated house orchestra, music lovers can enjoy listening to the masterpieces in the best possible conditions.

And with the Concertgebouw Circuit, Bruges quite literally becomes tangible as a classical music centre, because this art temple now opens its door to the public during the day. An original experience route leads you on a voyage of discovery through this wonderful building. Learn about its day-to-day running and be amazed by its outstanding acoustics. Marvel at the eye-opening contemporary architecture, be surprised by the fine collection of modern art or even try your own hand at a little sound art. The icing on the cake is the roof terrace on the seventh floor, from where you are rewarded with a magnificent view over the city.

♿ 📶 17 Concertgebouw Circuit

OPEN > Wednesday to Saturday, 2.00 p.m.-6.00 p.m., last admission: 5.30 p.m.; Sunday, 10.00 a.m.-12.30 p.m., last admission: 12.00 p.m. Guided tours (prior reservation necessary): Wednesday to Saturday at 3.00 p.m.

ADDITIONAL CLOSING DATES > 1/7 to 31/7. Sometimes (exceptionally) not open to the public; please check the website before planning your visit.

PRICE > €8; youngsters aged 6 to 25: €4; children younger than 6: free; guided tour: no additional charge

LANGUAGES > English, Dutch, French

INFO > 't Zand 34, tel. +32 (0)50 47 69 99, www.concertgebouwcircuit.be

🛜 01 08 Adornesdomein – Jeruzalemkapel (Adornes Estate – Jerusalem Chapel)

The Adornes domain consists of the 15th-century Jerusalem Chapel (a jewel of medieval architecture built by this rich merchant family), the Adornes mansion and a series of adjacent almshouses. In the multimedia museum, you step back in time to explore the life of Anselm Adornes and the Burgundian world in which he lived.

OPEN > 1/10 to 31/3: Monday to Saturday, 10.00 a.m.-5.00 p.m., 1/4 to 30/9: Monday to Friday, 10.00 a.m.-5.00 p.m., Saturday, 10.00 a.m.-6.00 p.m.

ADDITIONAL CLOSING DATES > All (Belgian) public holidays

PRICE > €7; 65+: €5; youngsters aged 7 to 25: €3.50; children under 7: free; family ticket: free from the third child

INFO > Peperstraat 3A, tel. +32 (0)50 33 88 83, www.adornes.org

02 Archeologiemuseum (Archaeological Museum)

This museum presents the unwritten history of Bruges. Its motto: feel your past beneath your feet. Discover the history of the city through different kinds of search and hands-on activities. A fascinating mix of archaeological finds, riddles, replicas and reconstructions shed light on daily life in times gone by, from the home to the workplace and from birth till death.

OPEN > Tuesday to Sunday, 9.30 a.m.-12.30 p.m. and 1.30 p.m.-5.00 p.m., last admission: 12.00 p.m. and 4.30 p.m. (open on Easter Monday and Whit Monday)

ADDITIONAL CLOSING DATES > 1/1, 10/5 (1.00 p.m.-5.00 p.m.) and 25/12

PRICE > €4; 65+ and youngsters aged 18 to 25: €3; children under 18: free

INFO > Mariastraat 36A, tel. +32 (0)50 44 87 43, www.museabrugge.be

03 Arentshuis

On the upper floor of this elegant city mansion with its picturesque garden (16th to 19th century) the oeuvre of the versatile British artist Frank Brangwyn (1867-1956) is on display on the top floor. Brangwyn was both a graphic artist and a painter, as well as a designer of carpets, furniture and ceramics. The ground floor is the setting for temporary plastic art exhibitions.

OPEN > Tuesday to Sunday, 9.30 a.m.-

5.00 p.m., last admission: 4.30 p.m. (open on Easter Monday and Whit Monday)

ADDITIONAL CLOSING DATES > 1/1, 10/5 (1.00 p.m.-5.00 p.m.) and 25/12

PRICE > €6; 65+ and youngsters aged 18 to 25: €5; children under 18: free; combination ticket with Groeninge Museum possible *(see page 62-63)*

INFO > Dijver 16, tel. +32 (0)50 44 87 43, www.museabrugge.be

🦽 01 Basiliek van het Heilig Bloed (Basilica of the Holy Blood)

The double church, dedicated to Our Lady and Saint Basil in the 12th century and a basilica since 1923, consists of a lower church that has maintained its Romanesque character and a neo-Gothic upper church, in which the relic of the Holy Blood is preserved. The treasury, with numerous valuable works of art, is also worth a visit.

OPEN > Daily, 9.30 a.m.-12.30 p.m. and 2.00 p.m.-5.30 p.m., last admission: 12.15 p.m. and 5.15 p.m. Veneration of the relic: daily, 11.30 a.m.-12.00 p.m. and 2.00 p.m.-4.00 p.m.

PRICE > Double church: free; treasury:

€2.50; children under 13: free

INFO > Burg 13, tel. +32 (0)50 33 67 92, www.holyblood.com

🦽 02 02 04 Begijnhof (Beguinage)

The 'Princely Beguinage Ten Wijngaarde' with its white-coloured house fronts and tranquil convent garden was founded in 1245. This little piece of world heritage was once the home of the beguines, emancipated lay-women who nevertheless led a pious and celibate life. Today the beguinage is inhabited by nuns of the Order of St. Benedict and several Bruges women who have decided to remain unmarried. In the Beguine's house, you can still get a good idea of what day-to-day life was like in the 17th century.

OPEN > Beguine's house: daily, 10.00 a.m.-5.00 p.m.; Beguinage: daily, 6.30 a.m.-6.30 p.m.

PRICE > Beguine's house: €2; 65+: €1.50; children aged 8 to 12 and students (on display of a valid student card): €1. Beguinage: free
INFO > Begijnhof 24-28-30, tel. +32 (0)50 33 00 11, www.monasteria.org

 Belfort (Belfry)

The most important of Bruges' towers stands 83 metres tall. It houses, amongst other things, a carillon. In the reception area, visitors can discover all kinds of interesting information about the history and working of this unique world-heritage protected belfry. Those who take on the challenge of climbing the tower can pause for a breather on the way up in the old treasury and also at the level of the impressive clock or in the carillonneur's chamber. Finally, after a tiring 366 steps, your efforts will

be rewarded with a breathtaking and unforgettable panoramic view of Bruges and its surroundings.
OPEN > Daily, 9.30 a.m.-6.00 p.m., last admission: 5.00 p.m. For safety reasons, only a limited number of people will be allowed to visit the tower at the same time. Reservations are not possible. Please consider a certain waiting period.
ADDITIONAL CLOSING DATES > 1/1, 10/5 (1.00 p.m.-6.00 p.m.) and 25/12
PRICE > €12; 65+ and youngsters aged 6 to 25: €10; children under 6: free
INFO > Markt 7, tel. +32 (0)50 44 87 43, www.museabrugge.be

Bezoekerscentrum Lissewege – Heiligenmuseum (Visitors Centre Lissewege – Saints' Museum)

The Visitors' Centre tells the story of 'the white village', which dates back through more than a thousand years of history. In the Saints' Museum, you can admire a remarkable collection of more than 130 antique statues of patron saints.
OPEN > During the long weekend of 1 May (28/4 to 1/5), on weekends in May

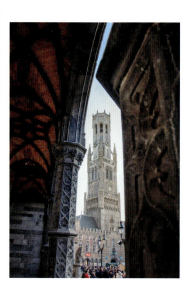

and June, during Ascension weekend (10/5 to 13/5), during Whit weekend (19/5 to 21/5), 1/7 to 15/9 and in the last two weekends of September (22/9-23/9 and 29/9-30/9): 2.00 p.m.-5.30 p.m.

PRICE > Saints' Museum: €2; children under 12: €1

INFO > Oude Pastoriestraat 5, Lissewege, tel. +32 (0)495 38 70 95, www.lissewege.be

🐬 📶 Boudewijn Seapark Bruges

In the Boudewijn Seapark, the dolphins steal the show with their spectacular leaps and the seals and sea lions perform the craziest tricks. But it is not only the sea mammals in this family park that will charm you, but also the twenty outdoor park attractions that offer guaranteed fun for young and old alike. Finally, *Bobo's Indoor* has twelve great indoor attractions, and *Bobo's Aqua Splash* provides 1,100 m² of wonderful water fun.

OPEN > During the period 31/3 to 30/9. During the Easter holidays (31/3 to 15/4) and weekends in April: 10.00

a.m.-5.00 p.m.; in May and June: daily, except on Wednesday, 10.00 a.m.-5.00 p.m.; in July and August: daily, 10.00 a.m.-6.00 p.m.; September: Saturday and Sunday, 10.00 a.m.-6.00 p.m. Consult the website for details of opening and availability during the autumn school holiday and winter period.

PRICE > €26.50; 65+ and children taller than 1 metre and under 12 years old: €22.50; children between 85 cm and 99 cm: €9.50; family ticket (2 adults + 2 children from 1-metre tall to 11 years of age): €83

INFO > Alfons De Baeckestraat 12, Sint-Michiels, tel. +32 (0)50 38 38 38, www.boudewijnseapark.be. Tickets at the amusement park entrance or at the tourist office 🅸 't Zand (Concert Hall).

📶 09 Brouwerij Bourgogne des Flandres (Brewery)

After an absence of 60 years, *Bourgogne des Flandres* is once again being brewed in Bruges. You can learn from the brewer himself how the beer is made, as well as tapping a digital glass in the interactive space. Or perhaps you can have a

bottle of the delicious brew personalized with your photo? The kids can amuse themselves with a fun treasure hunt. If you are still feeling thirsty after your visit, you can enjoy a glass of something pleasant on the romantic terrace overlooking the water.

OPEN > 1/9 to 30/6: Tuesday to Sunday and on all public holidays (including those that fall on a Monday), 10.00 a.m.-6.00 p.m.; 1/7 to 31/8: daily, 10.00 a.m.-6.00 p.m.; last guided tour starts at 5.10 p.m.

PRICE > Including one taster and an audio guide (available in 10 languages): €10.50; children aged 10 to 15: €5 (without taster); children under 10: free

INFO > Kartuizerinnenstraat 6, tel. +32 (0)50 33 54 26, www.bourgognedesflandres.be

📶 ⑩ Brouwerij De Halve Maan (Brewery)

This authentic brewery in the centre of Bruges is a family business with a tradition stretching back through six generations to 1856. This is where the Bruges city beer – the *Brugse Zot* – is brewed: a strong-tasting, high-fermentation beer based on malt, hops and special yeast. In 2016 a unique underground beer pipeline, some 3 km long, was laid from the brewery to the bottling plant in the suburbs.

OPEN > Sunday to Wednesday, 10.00 a.m.-6.00 p.m.; Thursday to Saturday, 10.00 a.m.-9.00 p.m. Guided tours: daily, on the hour, with the first tour at 11.00 a.m. and the last tour at 4.00 p.m. (5.00 p.m. on Thursday to Saturday); XL-tour with a tasting of three special beers: daily, 2.00 p.m.-3.30 p.m.

ADDITIONAL CLOSING DATES > 1/1, 24/12 and 25/12

PRICE > Including taster: €10; children aged 6 to 12: €5; children under 6: free; XL-Tour: €19

LANGUAGES > English, Dutch, French. XL-Tour in English and Dutch.

INFO > Walplein 26, tel. +32 (0)50 44 42 22, www.halvemaan.be

📶 ⑫ Bruges Beer Experience

Discover in an interactive way everything you ever wanted to know about the raw ingredients of beer, the brewing process, food pairing, beer in Bruges, trappist and abbey beers, etc. Children follow the Kids Tour, which tells the story of the

Bruges bear. Would you just like to sample some beers? The tasting room and its 16 different kinds of beer is open to everyone and has a great view over the Market Square.

OPEN > Daily, 10.00 a.m.-5.00 p.m. (tasting room until 6.30 p.m.)

ADDITIONAL CLOSING DATES > 1/1 and 25/12

PRICE > Including iPad Mini with headphones (available in 11 languages): €15 (with 3 beer samplings) or €9 (without beer samples); children aged 5 to 12: €6; family ticket (2 adults + max. 3 children): €32 (with beer samples) or €20 (without beer samples)

INFO > Breidelstraat 3 (top floor former Post Office), tel. +32 (0)496 76 45 54, www.mybeerexperience.com

♿ 🛜 03 07 13 Brugse Vrije (Liberty of Bruges)

From this mansion, the countryside in a wide area around the city was once governed. The building functioned as a court of justice between 1795 and 1984. Today, the City Archive (amongst other things) is housed here. They safeguard Bruges' written memory. The premises also boast an old assize court and a renaissance hall with a monumental 16th-century timber, marble and alabaster fireplace made by Lanceloot Blondeel.

OPEN > Daily, 9.30 a.m.-12.30 p.m. and 1.30 p.m.-5.00 p.m., last admission: 12.00 p.m. and 4.30 p.m.

ADDITIONAL CLOSING DATES > 1/1, 10/5 (1.00 p.m.-5.00 p.m.) and 25/12

PRICE > Including City Hall: €6; 65+ and youngsters aged 18 to 25: €5; children under 18: free. Tickets are sold in the City Hall.

APP > You can visit the Liberty of Bruges with the Xplore Bruges app (www.xplore bruges.be)

INFO > Burg 11A, tel. +32 (0)50 44 87 43, www.museabrugge.be

🛜 14 Choco-Story (Chocolate Museum)

The museum dips its visitors in the history of cocoa and chocolate. From the Maya and the Spanish conquistadores to the chocolate connoisseurs of today. Children can explore the museum via a fun chocolate search game. Chocolates are made by hand and sampled on the premises. In 2015, the museum opened a thematic Choco-Jungle Bar at Vlamingstraat 31, just a 5-minute walk away.

OPEN > Daily, 10.00 a.m.-5.00 p.m. (1/7 to 31/8, until 6.00 p.m.), last admission: 45 min. before closing time

ADDITIONAL CLOSING DATES > 1/1, 8/1 to 12/1 and 25/12

PRICE > €8; 65+ and students aged 12 to 26: €7; children aged 6 to 11: €5; children

under 6: free; several combination tickets possible *(see page 74)*
LANGUAGES > Free audio guide available in German, Spanish and Italian. There are info-boards in Dutch, French and English.
INFO > Wijnzakstraat 2, tel. +32 (0)50 61 22 37, www.choco-story.be

Cozmix – Volkssterrenwacht (Public Observatory) Beisbroek

Admire the beauty of the sun, moon and planets in glorious closeup, thanks to a powerful telescope. In the planetarium more than seven thousand stars are projected onto the interior of the dome. Spectacular video images take you on a journey through the mysteries of the universe. The artistic planet-pathway (with sculptures by Jef Claerhout) will complete your voyage of discovery into outer space.
OPEN > Wednesday and Sunday, 2.30 p.m.-6.00 p.m.; Friday, 8.00 p.m.-10.00 p.m. Planetarium shows on Wednesday and Sunday at 3.00 p.m. and 4.30 p.m. and on Friday at

8.30 p.m. Extended opening hours and extra planetarium shows during Belgian school holidays; please consult the website.
ADDITIONAL CLOSING DATES > 1/1 and 25/12
PRICE > €6; youngsters aged 4 to 17: €5
LANGUAGES > Shows in languages other than Dutch on Wednesday at 4.30 p.m.: first and third weeks of the month in French, second, fourth and fifth weeks in English
INFO > Zeeweg 96, Sint-Andries, tel. +32 (0)50 39 05 66, www.cozmix.be

19 Diamantmuseum Brugge (Bruges Diamond Museum)

Did you know that the technique of cutting diamonds was first applied in Bruges almost 550 years ago? The Bruges Diamond Museum tells this story in a series of fascinating exhibition displays. There is a live demonstration of diamond cutting each day and in the diamond laboratory, microscopes and other equipment allow visitors, both young and old alike, to discover the true beauty of diamonds in all their many facets.

OPEN > Daily, 10.30 a.m.-5.30 p.m. Cutting demonstrations: daily, 12.15 p.m.; during the weekends, (Belgian) school holidays and 1/4 to 31/10: extra demonstration at 3.15 p.m. (visitors need to be present 15 minutes in advance)
ADDITIONAL CLOSING DATES > 1/1, 8/1 to 19/1 and 25/12
PRICE > €8 (without cutting demonstration) or €11 (with cutting demonstration); 65+, students (on display of a valid student card) and children aged 6 to 12: €7 (without cutting demonstration) or €10 (with cutting demonstration); children under 6: free; family ticket (2 adults + 2 children): €21 (without cutting demonstration) or €33 (with cutting demonstration); a combination ticket is possible *(see page 74)*
LANGUAGES > Demonstrations in 7 languages
INFO > Katelijnestraat 43, tel. +32 (0)50 34 20 56, www.diamondmuseum.be

🎧 21 Foltermuseum De Oude Steen (Torture Museum)

In what is probably the oldest stone building in Bruges, you can discover a remarkable and spine-chilling collection of instruments of torture and learn about the history of law, order and justice in the city, including the use of torture and the punishments inflicted on the guilty. You will get a clear picture of the harsh practice of medieval law, where the ends of Lady Justice justified the means.
OPEN > Daily, 10.30 a.m.-6.30 p.m. (1/7 to 15/9, until 9.00 p.m.)

PRICE > €8; 60+: €7; students: €6; children under 6: free; family ticket (2 adults + 3 children under 16): €20
INFO > Wollestraat 29, tel. +32 (0)50 73 41 34, www.torturemuseum.be

♿ 🎧 🅼 08 22 Frietmuseum (Belgian Fries Museum)

This didactical museum sketches the history of the potato, Belgian fries and the various sauces and dressings that accompany this most delicious and most famous of Belgian comestibles. The museum is housed in the Saaihalle, one of Bruges' most attractive buildings. Show your entrance ticket and enjoy a €0.40 discount on a portion of fries.
OPEN > Daily, 10.00 a.m.-5.00 p.m., last admission: 4.15 p.m.
ADDITIONAL CLOSING DATES > 1/1, 8/1 to 12/1 and 25/12
PRICE > €7; 65+ and students aged to 12 to 26: €6; children aged 6 to 11: €5; children under 6: free; several combination tickets possible *(see page 74)*
LANGUAGES > Free audio guide available in 6 languages
INFO > Vlamingstraat 33, tel. +32 (0)50 34 01 50, www.frietmuseum.be

07 23 Gentpoort (Gate of Ghent)

The Gate of Ghent is one of four remaining medieval city gates. An entrance for foreigners, a border with the outside world for the townspeople of Bruges. The gate was a part of the city's defences as well as a passageway for the movement of produce and merchandise. The Ghent Gate is at its most beautiful in the evening, when it is quite literally in the spotlight.

OPEN > Tuesday to Sunday, 9.30 a.m.-12.30 p.m. and 1.30 p.m.-5.00 p.m., last admission: 12.00 p.m. and 4.30 p.m. (open on Easter Monday and Whit Monday)

ADDITIONAL CLOSING DAYS > 1/1, 10/5 (1.00 p.m.-5 p.m.) and 25/12

PRICE > €4; 65+ and youngsters aged 18 to 25: €3; children under 18: free

INFO > Gentpoortvest, tel. +32 (0)50 44 87 43, www.museabrugge.be

24 Gezellemuseum (Gezelle Museum)

This literary and biographical museum about the life of Guido Gezelle (1830-1899), one of Flanders' most famous poets, was established in the house where he was born, situated in a peaceful working-class district of the city. In addition to displays about his life and works, there are also temporary presentations about (literary) art. Next to the house there is a romantic garden, with Jan Fabre's *The Man Who Gives a Light* as the main attraction.

OPEN > Tuesday to Sunday, 9.30 a.m.-12.30 p.m. and 1.30 p.m.-5.00 p.m., last admission: 12.00 p.m. and 4.30 p.m. (open on Easter Monday and Whit Monday)

ADDITIONAL CLOSING DATES > 1/1, 10/5 (1.00 p.m.-5.00 p.m.) and 25/12

PRICE > €4; 65+ and youngsters aged 18 to 25: €3; children under 18: free

INFO > Rolweg 64, tel. +32 (0)50 44 87 43, www.museabrugge.be

♿ 📶 25 Groeningemuseum (Groeninge Museum)

The Groeninge Museum provides a varied overview of the history of Belgian visual art, with the world-renowned Flemish primitives as a highlight. In this museum you can see, amongst other masterpieces, *Madonna with Canon Joris Van der Paele* by Jan van Eyck and the *Moreel Triptych* by Hans Mem-

07 Heilige Magdalenakerk (St. Magdalene's Church)

The St. Magdalene's Church, built in the mid-19th century, was one of the earliest neo-Gothic churches on the European mainland. This style of architecture, first made popular in England, was brought to Bruges by British immigrants. That is how the neo-Gothic appeared in the streets of Bruges quite early. Inside the church you can make your acquaintance with YOT, an organization that explores the meaning of the Christian tradition in modern society.

OPEN > 1/1 to 31/3: Friday to Monday, 3.00 p.m.-6.00 p.m.; 1/4 to 30/9: daily, 11.00 a.m.-6.00 p.m.; 1/10 to 31/12: daily, 1.00 p.m.-6.00 p.m. The church is not open for visitors during liturgical services.
ADDITIONAL CLOSING DATES > 1/1, 24/12, 25/12 and 31/12
PRICE > Free
INFO > Corner Stalijzerstraat and Schaarstraat, tel. +32 (0)50 33 68 18, www.yot.be

ling. You will also marvel at the top 18th and 19th-century neoclassical pieces, masterpieces of Flemish Expressionism and post-war modern art.
OPEN > Tuesday to Sunday, 9.30 a.m.-5.00 p.m., last admission: 4.30 p.m. (open on Easter Monday and Whit Monday)
ADDITIONAL CLOSING DATES > 1/1, 10/5 (1.00 p.m.-5.00 p.m.) and 25/12
PRICE > Including Arentshuis: €12; 65+ and youngsters aged 18 to 25: €10; children under 18: free; a combination ticket is possible *(see page 74)*
INFO > Dijver 12, tel. +32 (0)50 44 87 43, www.museabrugge.be

26 Gruuthusemuseum (Gruuthuse Museum)

By spring 2019 (subject to amendment), you will once again be able to admire this luxurious city palace of the lords of Gruuthuse in all its magnificent glory. After extensive restoration and renovation, visitors will once again be able to learn more about Bruges and enjoy the outstanding collections of tapestries, lace, sculpture, furniture and silver.
INFO > Dijver 17, tel. +32 (0)50 44 87 43, www.museabrugge.be

Historium Bruges

Film set decors, music and special effects take you back to a day in 1435. The attraction reconstructs, amongst other things, the Water Halls, a huge storage depot that once stood for five centuries on the Market Square. Don't forget to try the VR Experience, which uses the wonder of virtual reality to immerse you in 15th century Bruges. Or follow the brand-new Family Trail: an interactive route full of fun for kids. All rounded off with a visit

to the Duvelorium Grand Beer Café and its panoramic terrace.

OPEN > Daily, 10.00 a.m.-6.00 p.m., last admission: 5.00 p.m.

PRICE > Including audio guide (available in 10 languages): €14; students: €10; children aged 3 to 12: €7.50; VR Experience: €5 or an additional €3.50 if you also visit the Historium; all-in ticket (visit Historium, VR Experience and a drink of your choice in the Duvelorium): €19.50; family ticket (2 adults + 2 children): €38; a combination ticket is possible *(see page 74)*

INFO > Markt 1, tel. +32 (0)50 27 03 11, www.historium.be

♿ ③⓪ Kantcentrum (Lace Centre)

The Lace Centre has been housed in the renovated old lace school of the Sisters of the Immaculate Conception. The story of Bruges lace is told in the lace museum on the ground floor. Multimedia installations and testimonies from international lace experts help to explain the various different types of lace and their geographical origin, and focus on the lace industry and lace education in Bruges. Demonstrations and

various courses are organized in the lace workshop on the second floor.

OPEN > Monday to Saturday, 9.30 a.m.-5.00 p.m., last admission: 4.30 p.m. Demonstrations: Monday to Saturday, 2.00 p.m.-5.00 p.m.

ADDITIONAL CLOSING DATES > All (Belgian) public holidays

PRICE > €6; 65+ and youngsters aged 12 to 26: €5; children under 12: free; a combination ticket is possible *(see page 74)*

INFO > Balstraat 16, tel. +32 (0)50 33 00 72, www.kantcentrum.eu

📶 ③① Lumina Domestica (Lamp Museum)

The museum contains the world's largest collection of lamps and lights. More than six thousand antiques tell the complete story of interior lighting, from the torch and paraffin lamp to the light bulb and LED. The small detour into the world of luminous animals and plants is particularly interesting. In this way you can discover, for example, the light mysteries of the glow-worm, the lantern fish and the small Chinese lantern.

OPEN > Daily, 10.00 a.m.-5.00 p.m. (1/7 to 31/8, until 6.00 p.m.), last admission: 45 min. before closing time

ADDITIONAL CLOSING DATES > 1/1, 8/1 to 12/1 and 25/12

PRICE > €7; 65+ and students aged 12 to 26: €6; children aged 6 to 11: €5; children under 6: free; several combination tickets possible *(see page 74)*

INFO > Wijnzakstraat 2, tel. +32 (0)50 61 22 37, www.luminadomestica.be

Onze-Lieve-Vrouw-Bezoekingkerk Lissewege (Church of Our Lady of Visitation)

The 13th-century brick Church of Our Lady of Visitation is a textbook example of 'coastal Gothic'. Its interior has a miraculous statue of the Virgin Mary (1625), an exceptional organ case and a beautifully sculptured rood loft and pulpit (1652). Anyone who makes the effort to climb all 264 steps of the squat, flat-topped tower will be rewarded with a panoramic view over the polders towards Bruges.

OPEN > Church: 1/5 to 30/9: daily, 9.00 a.m.-6.00 p.m.; 1/10 to 30/4: daily, 10.00 a.m.-4.00 p.m.

Tower: during the weekends 23/6-24/6, 30/6-1/7, 1/9-2/9, 8/9-9/9 and 1/7 to 31/8: daily, 2.00 p.m.-5.30 p.m., last admission: 5.00 p.m.

PRICE > Church: free. Tower: €2; children under 12: €0.50

INFO > Onder de Toren, Lissewege, tel. +32 (0)50 54 45 44 (church), +32 (0)487 49 92 14 (tower), www.lissewege.be

Onze-Lieve-Vrouwekerk (Church of Our Lady)

The 115.5-metres high brick tower of the Church of Our Lady is a perfect illustration of the craftsmanship of Bruges' artisans. The church displays a valuable art collection: Michelangelo's world-famous *Madonna and Child*, countless paintings, 13th-century painted sepulchres and the tombs of Mary of Burgundy and Charles the Bold. The choir was renovated in 2015 and the remarkable church interior can now once again be admired in all its splendour.

OPEN > Monday to Saturday, 9.30 a.m.-5.00 p.m.; Sunday and Holy Days, 1.30 p.m.-5.00 p.m., last admission: 4.30 p.m. The church and the museum are not open to visitors during nuptial and funeral masses. Useful to know: at the moment, large-scale renovation works are still being carried out, so

the church is only partially accessible and many works of art cannot be viewed.

ADDITIONAL CLOSING DATES > Museum: 1/1, 10/5 and 25/12

PRICE > Church: free. Museum: €6; 65+ and youngsters aged 18 to 25: €5; children under 18: free. There is a reduced entrance fee during the restoration work.

INFO > Mariastraat, tel. +32 (0)50 44 87 43, www.museabrugge.be

16 34 Onze-Lieve-Vrouw-ter-Potterie (Our Lady of the Pottery)

This hospital dates back to the 13th century, when nuns took on the care of pilgrims, travellers and the sick. In the 15th century, it evolved towards a more modern type of home for the elderly. The hospital wards with their valuable collection of works of art, monastic and religious relics and a range of objects used in nursing have been converted into a museum. The Gothic church with its baroque interior can also be visited.

OPEN > Tuesday to Sunday, 9.30 a.m.-12.30 p.m. and 1.30 p.m.-5.00 p.m., last admission: 12.00 p.m. and 4.30 p.m. (open on Easter Monday and Whit Monday)

ADDITIONAL CLOSING DATES > 1/1, 10/5 (1.00 p.m.-5.00 p.m.) and 25/12

PRICE > Church: free. Museum: €6; 65+ and youngsters aged 18 to 25: €5; children under 18: free

INFO > Potterierei 79B, tel. +32 (0)50 44 87 43, www.museabrugge.be

17 Onze-Lieve-Vrouw-van-Blindekenskapel (Chapel of our Lady of the Blind)

The original wooden Chapel of Our Lady of Blindekens was erected in 1305 as an expression of gratitude to Our Lady after the Battle of Mons-en-Pévèle (1304). The current chapel dates from 1651. In order to fulfil the 'Bruges promise', made on the field of battle, the Blindekens procession has paraded through the streets of the city on 15th August every year since

1305. As part of the procession, the women of Bruges donate a candle (of 18 kilograms) to the Church of Onze-Lieve-Vrouw-ter-Potterie.

OPEN > Daily, 9.30 a.m.-6.00 p.m.
PRICE > Free
INFO > Kreupelenstraat 8, tel. +32 (0)50 32 76 60 of +32 (0)50 33 68 41

04 36 Expo Picasso

At the historic Oud Sint-Jan (Old St. John) site, you can view more than 400 original works of art by the great Spanish masters Pablo Picasso and Joan Miró. In addition to these permanent exhibitions, the 19th-century infirmary wards are also the setting each year for prestigious temporary exhibitions.

OPEN > Daily, 10.00 a.m.-6.00 p.m.
ADDITIONAL CLOSING DATES > 1/1 to 31/1

PRICE > €10; 65+ and youngsters aged 6 to 18: €8; children under 6: free
INFO > Site Oud Sint-Jan, Mariastraat 38, tel. +32 (0)50 47 61 00, www.xpo-center-bruges.be

37 Museum-Gallery Xpo Salvador Dalí

In the Cloth Halls, you can admire a fantastic collection of world-famous graphics and statues by the great artist Dalí. They are all authentic works of art that are described in the *Catalogues Raisonnés*, which details Salvador Dalí's oeuvre. The collection is presented in a sensational *Daliesque* décor of mirrors, gold and *shocking pink*.

OPEN > Daily, 10.00 a.m.-6.00 p.m. (24/12 and 31/12, until 3.30 p.m.)
ADDITIONAL CLOSING DATES > 1/1 and 25/12

PRICE > €10; 65+, youngsters aged 13 to 18 and students (on display of a valid student card): €8; children under 13: free
LANUAGES > Audio guide available in 3 languages: €2
INFO > Markt 7, tel. +32 (0)50 33 83 44, www.dali-interart.be

⌔ Seafront Zeebrugge

In the unique setting of the former fish auction hall in Zeebrugge you will learn about the Belgian fishing industry and the thriving world port of Bruges. Experience what seaside tourism was like in the past and also in the present. Take on the role of the captain of the West-Hinder lightship or pretend you are a sailor on an authentic Russian submarine. Seafront also has a number of fascinating permanent exhibitions, like *Fish from the boat right onto your plate*, *Fish stories*, *For freedom* and *Besieged Coast, Occupied Harbour – Zeebrugge & WWI*.

OPEN > Daily, 10.00 a.m.-5.00 p.m. (1/7 to 31/8, until 6.00 p.m); adapted opening hours in November and December: consult the website

ADDITIONAL CLOSING DATES > 1/1, 8/1 to 26/1 and 25/12

PRICE > Including visit to exhibitions: €13.50; 60+ and students (on display of a valid student card): €11.50; children under 12: €9.50; children up to 1 metre (accompanied by an adult): free

INFO > Vismijnstraat 7, Zeebrugge, tel. +32 (0)50 55 14 15, www.seafront.be

19 Sint-Annakerk (St. Anne's Church)

This simple Gothic single-nave church, built in the 17th century, surprises with the opulence of its rich Baroque interior – the result of donations by wealthy local patrons. Admire the intricacy of the marble rood-screen, the rich wooden panelling with inset confessional booths, the canvases of Jan Garemijn and the largest single painting in all Bruges.

OPEN > 1/1 to 31/3: Friday to Monday, 3.00 p.m.-6.00 p.m.; 1/4 to 30/9: daily, 11.00 a.m.-6.00 p.m.; 1/10 to 31/12: daily, 1.00 p.m.-6.00 p.m. The church is not open to visitors during liturgical services.

ADDITIONAL CLOSING DATES > 1/1, 24/12, 25/12 and 31/12

PRICE > Free

INFO > Sint-Annaplein, tel. +32 (0)50 34 87 05, www.sintdonatianusbrugge.be

20 Sint-Gilliskerk (St. Giles' Church)

In this church, the only one in the city centre with a tower clock, many of the great Bruges artists have been buried. These include Hans Memling, Lance-

loot Blondeel and Pieter Pourbus. The church originally dates from the 13th century, but was extensively rebuilt in the 15th century. The exterior is a fine example of the robust Brick Gothic style, while the interior has a more refined 19th-century neo-Gothic look.

OPEN > 1/1 to 31/3: Friday to Monday, 3.00 p.m.-6.00 p.m.; 1/4 to 30/9: daily, 11.00 a.m.- 6.00 p.m.; 1/10 to 31/12: daily, 1.00 p.m.-6.00 p.m. The church is not open to visitors during religious services.

ADDITIONAL CLOSING DATES > 1/1, 24/12, 25/12 and 31/12

PRICE > Free

INFO > Sint-Gilliskerkstraat, tel. +32 (0)50 34 87 05, www.sintdonatianus brugge.be

22 Sint-Jakobskerk (St. James's Church)

In the middle of the 13th century, the modest St. James's Chapel was elevated to the status of a parish church. During the 15th century, this simple house of prayer was extended to its current size. The church is now famous for its rich collection of art treasures, donated by wealthy local people living nearby, and for its fine examples of funerary art.

OPEN > 1/1 to 31/3: Friday to Monday, 3.00 p.m.-6.00 p.m.; 1/4 to 30/9: daily, 11.00 a.m.-6.00 p.m.; 1/10 to 31/12: daily, 1.00 p.m.-6.00 p.m. The church is not open to visitors during religious services.

ADDITIONAL CLOSING DATES > 1/1, 24/12, 25/12 and 31/12

PRICE > Free

APP > You can visit the church using the Xplore Bruges app (www.xplore bruges.be)

INFO > Sint-Jakobsplein, tel. +32 (0)50 33 68 41, www.sintdonatianusbrugge.be

♿ 📶 38 Sint-Janshospitaal (Saint John's Hospital)

Saint John's Hospital has an eight hundred-year-old history of caring for pilgrims, travellers, the poor and the sick. Visit the medieval wards, as well as the church and the chapel, and marvel at the impressive collection of archives, art works, medical instruments and six paintings by Hans Memling. Also worth a visit: the Diksmuide attic, the old dormitory, the adjoining custodian's room and the pharmacy.

OPEN > Museum: Tuesday to Sunday, 9.30 a.m.-5.00 p.m. Pharmacy: Tuesday to Sunday, 9.30 a.m.-12.30 p.m. and 1.30 p.m.-5.00 p.m., last admission both: 4.30 p.m. (both open on Easter Monday and Whit Monday)

ADDITIONAL CLOSING DATES > 1/1, 10/5 (1.00 p.m.-5.00 p.m.) and 25/12

PRICE > Including visit to the pharmacy: €12; 65+ and youngsters aged 18 to 25: €10; children under 18: free

APP > You can learn more about the six works of Hans Memling via the Xplore Bruges app (www.xplorebruges.be)

INFO > Mariastraat 38, tel. +32 (0)50 44 87 43, www.museabrugge.be

39 Sint-Janshuismolen (Mill)

Windmills have graced Bruges' ramparts ever since the construction of the outer city wall at the end of the 13th century. Today four specimens are left on Kruisvest. The Sint-Janshuis Mill, built in 1770 and still occupying its original site, is the only mill still grinding flour and the only mill open to visitors.

OPEN > 1/4 to 30/9: Tuesday to Sunday, 9.30 a.m.-12.30 p.m. and 1.30 p.m.-5.00 p.m., last admission: 12.00 p.m. and 4.30 p.m. (open on Easter Monday and Whit Monday).

ADDITIONAL CLOSING DATE > 10/5 (1.00 p.m.-5.00 p.m.)

PRICE > €4; 65+ and youngsters aged 18 to 25: €3; children under 18: free

INFO > Kruisvest, tel. +32 (0)50 44 87 43, www.museabrugge.be

23 Sint-Salvators-kathedraal (Saint Saviour's Cathedral)

Bruges' oldest parish church (12th-15th century) has amongst its treasures a rood loft with an organ, medieval tombs, Brussels tapestries and a rich collection of Flemish paintings (14th-18th century). The treasure-chamber displays, amongst others, paintings by Dieric Bouts, Hugo van der Goes and other Flemish primitives.

OPEN > Cathedral: Monday to Friday, 10.00 a.m.-1.00 p.m. and 2.00 p.m.-5.30 p.m.; Saturday, 10.00 a.m.-1.00 p.m. and 2.00 p.m.-3.30 p.m.; Sunday, 11.30 a.m.-12.00 p.m. and 2.00 p.m.-5.00 p.m.; the cathedral is not open to visitors during liturgical services. Treasury: daily (except Saturday), 2.00 p.m.- 5.00 p.m.

ADDITIONAL CLOSING DATES > Cathedral (afternoon) and treasury (all day): 1/1, 10/5, 24/12 and 25/12

PRICE > Cathedral and Treasury: free

INFO > Steenstraat, tel. +32 (0)50 33 61 88, www.sintsalvator.be

24 Sint-Walburgakerk (St. Walburga's Church)

In 1619, a Bruges lay brother, Pieter Huyssens, was commissioned to build a prestigious church that expressed the values and beliefs of the Jesuits. The result was the St. Walburga's Church, which is the most richly decorated church in pure Baroque style in Bruges. Admire its dynamic facade, its many interior architectural details and the elaborately decorated church furniture.

OPEN > 1/1 to 31/3: Friday to Monday, 3.00 p.m.-6.00 p.m.; 1/4 to 30/9: daily, 11.00 a.m.-6.00 p.m.; 1/10 to 31/12: daily, 1.00 p.m.-6.00 p.m.

ADDITIONAL CLOSING DATES > 1/1, 24/12, 25/12 and 31/12

PRICE > Free

INFO > Sint-Maartensplein

41 Schuttersgilde Sint-Sebastiaan (Saint Sebastian's Archers Guild)

The Guild of Saint Sebastian is an archers' guild that has already been in existence for more than 600 years, which is unprecedented anywhere in the world.

The members of this longbow guild are exclusively male, with two notable exceptions: Queen Mathilde of Belgium and the Queen of England. A visit includes the royal chamber, the chapel chamber and the garden.

OPEN > 1/10 to 31/3: Tuesday to Thursday and Saturday, 2.00 p.m.-5.00 p.m., 1/4 to 30/9: Tuesday to Thursday, 10.00 a.m.-12.00 p.m. and Saturday, 2.00 p.m.-5.00 p.m. Please note: do not be put off by the closed door; you always need to ring the bell to gain access.

ADDITIONAL CLOSING DATES > All (Belgian) holidays and 14/6 to 20/6

PRICE > €3

INFO > Carmersstraat 174, tel. +32 (0)50 33 16 26, www.sebastiaansgilde.be

♿ 🛜 08 42 Stadhuis (City Hall)

Bruges' City Hall (1376-1420) is one of the oldest in the Low Countries. It is from here that the city has been governed for more than 600 years. An absolute masterpiece is the Gothic Hall, with its late 19th-century murals and polychrome vault. In the historic chamber next door, original documents and artefacts are used to evoke the history of the city's administration through the centuries. On the ground floor, the structural development of the Burg square and the City Hall is illustrated.

OPEN > Daily, 9.30 a.m.-5.00 p.m., last admission: 4.30 p.m. The Gothic Hall and the historic chamber are not open to visitors during weddings.

ADDITIONAL CLOSING DATES > 1/1, 10/5 (1.00 p.m.-5.00 p.m.) and 25/12

PRICE > Including Liberty of Bruges: €6; 65+ and youngsters aged 18 to 25: €5; children under 18: free

APP > Visit the City Hall with the free app Xplore Bruges (www.xplorebruges.be)

LANGUAGES > Free audio guide available in 5 languages
INFO > Burg 12, tel. +32 (0)50 44 87 43, www.museabrugge.be

🛜 ㊹ Volkskundemuseum (Museum of Folk Life)

These renovated 17th century, single room dwellings accommodate, amongst other things, a classroom, a millinery, a pharmacy, a confectionery shop, a grocery shop and an authentic bedroom interior. The upper floor is used for temporary exhibitions. You can relax in the museum inn, 'De Zwarte Kat' (The Black Cat) or in the garden, where you can try out traditional folk and children's games on the terrace.
OPEN > Museum and inn: Tuesday to Sunday, 9.30 a.m.-5.00 p.m., last admission: 4.30 p.m. (open on Easter Monday and Whit Monday)

ADDITIONAL CLOSING DATES > 1/1, 10/5 (1.00 p.m.-5.00 p.m.) and 25/12
PRICE > €6; 65+ and youngsters aged 18 to 25: €5; children under 18: free; a combination ticket is possible
(see page 74)
INFO > Balstraat 43, tel. +32 (0)50 44 87 43, www.museabrugge.be

MAKE THE MOST OF IT!

» Museum Pass

With the Museum Pass you can visit the different Musea Brugge locations (www.museabrugge.be) as often as you like for just €28. Youngsters aged 18 to 25 pay just €22. The pass is valid for three consecutive days and can be purchased at all Musea Brugge locations (except for the Liberty of Bruges and the Church of Our Lady), the **i** Markt (Historium) and at the **i** 't Zand (Concert Hall).

» Discount cards with your stay

Enjoy a discount on the admission fees to various museums, attractions and other sites of interest using the free Discover Bruges card that you get whenever you stay in one of the hotels affiliated with Hotels Regio Bruges vzw (www.discoverbruges.com) or the free Bruges Advantage City Card that you get whenever you spend a night at one of the B&B's affiliated to the Gilde der Brugse Gastenverblijven vzw (www.brugge-bedandbreakfast.com).

» Combination ticket Historium/Groeninge Museum

Experience the golden century of Bruges in the Historium, with the painting of *Madonna with Canon Joris van der Paele* by Jan van Eyck as your leitmotif. Then see the masterpiece itself in the Groeninge Museum, along with the great works of many others of the so-called Flemish primitives. This €22 combination ticket is only available in the Historium.

» Combination ticket Choco-Story/Diamond Museum

Combine a tasty visit to Choco-Story with a dazzling look at the Diamond Museum. This combination ticket costs €17 (including diamond-cutting demonstration) or €14 (without demonstration). For sale at the above-mentioned museums and at the tourist office **i** 't Zand (Concert Hall).

» Combination ticket Choco-Story/Lumina Domestica/Belgian Fries Museum

Visit these three museums at reduced rates.

- » Combination ticket Choco-Story/Belgian Fries Museum: €13; 65+ and students: €11; children aged 6 to 11: €8; children under 6: free
- » Combination ticket Choco-Story/Lumina Domestica: €10; 65+ and students: €9; children aged 6 to 11: €7; children under 6: free
- » Combination ticket (3 museums): €15; 65+ and students: €13; children aged 6 to 11: €10; children under 6: free. These combination tickets are for sale at the above-mentioned museums and at the tourist office **i** 't Zand (Concert Hall).

» Combination ticket Lace Centre/Museum of Folk Life

The Lace Centre has a display of lace from the collection of Musea Brugge, which perfectly complements the lacework that can be admired in the Museum of Folk Life. Combination ticket: €10, only on sale in both museums.

Culture and events

Concert Hall

The city's high-quality cultural life flourishes as never before. Devotees of modern architecture stand in awe of the Concertgebouw (Concert Hall) whilst enjoying an international top concert or an exhilarating dance performance. Romantic souls throng the elegant City Theatre for an unforgettable night. Jazz enthusiasts feel at home at Art Centre De KAAP | De Werf, whereas the MaZ is the place to be for young people.

Bruges Triennial 2018

Liquid City

Contemporary art and architecture route in Bruges

5/5/2018 – 16/9/2018 – www.triennalebrugge.be

Triennial 2015

Song Dong
Wu Wei Er Wei (Doing Nothing Doing)

In 2018, the Triennial will return to Bruges for the second time. Held once every three years, this artistic route, with surprising installations by celebrated artists and architects, is spread right across the city centre. The Triennial explores the future of a city like Bruges, and hopes to serve as safe point of reference. Bruges as a fluid city, open and committed, a motor of social, cultural and political change.

Bruges as a breeding ground for innovation and renewal. Just like the city's medieval citizens, who first gave Bruges its shape and form, today's residents also share common dreams for the further development of life in Bruges. Bruges Triennial 2018 seeks to stimulate interaction and lay new and solid foundations for the future of the city. A liquid city, quite literally surrounded by water, but also liquid in a metaphorical sense, as a city in constant and flowing artistic movement, sometimes storm-tossed, sometimes peaceful and calm.

Also read the interviews with the curators of the Bruges Triennial 2018 on pages 104-107 and 112-115.

1. Jarosław Kozakiewicz [PL], BRUG
2. Wesley Meuris [BE], UrbanModeL
3. Renato Nicolodi [BE], ACHERON I
4. NLÉ — Kunlé Adeyemi [NG-NL], MFS III - Minne Floating School
5. OBBA [KR], The Floating Island
6. Roxy Paine [USA], Ground Fault
7. John Powers [USA], Lanchals
8. raumlabor [DE], House of Time, Site Pakhuizen
9. Rotor [BE], The Mitten Crab Project
10. Ruimteveldwerk [BE], G.O.D.
11. Tomás Saraceno [AR], Bruges Aerocene Tower
12. selgascano [ES], URB EGG
13. Monir Shahroudy Farmanfarmaian [IR], Fountain of Life
14. StudioKCA [USA], Skyscraper [the Bruges Whale]
15. Peter Van Driessche — Atelier4 [BE], Infinity^{23}

A. Poortersloge (1), expo (9) (11)
B. Grootseminarie, expo Architecture de l'Errance

What's on the programme in 2018?

The following list summarizes the most important events in Bruges. You can also pick up a free monthly events calendar from the info-offices **i** Markt (Historium), Stationsplein (station) and 't Zand (Concert Hall). The last office also sells tickets for events (and lots of other activities). For a fully detailed events calendar, you can always surf to www.visitbruges.be.

January

Bach Academie
24/1/2018 – 28/1/2018

In the world of Bach, without radio, CDs or streaming, the same music was often played repeatedly on various occasions. In other words, the composers liked to reuse their 'greatest hits'.
In the eighth Bruges Bach Academy you can not only discover how Bach reworked his own music and the music of others, but also how he inspired other adventurous musicians to stretch their own artistic boundaries.
INFO > www.concertgebouw.be *(You can read more about Bach and Early Music in the interview with Albert Edelman on pages 120-123)*

INNOVATIVE, MEDIEVAL BOOK PRINTING
1/3/2018 to 3/6/2018

In the 15th century, Bruges was famous for its book printing. In particular, the books printed by Colard Mansion were much in demand. Mansion was a constant innovator and was the first, for example, to introduce the use of engravings in printed books. Learn more about his life and oeuvre in the exhibition *Haute Lecture by Colard Mansion. Innovation in text and images in medieval Bruges* in the Groeninge Museum.

INFO > www.museabrugge.be

Wintervonken (Winter Sparks)

26/1/2018 and 27/1/2018

Winter Sparks brings warmth and conviviality to the Burg square. The fifth edition of this winter festival once again guarantees scintillating street theatre, atmospheric concerts and heartwarming fire installations.

INFO > www.wintervonken.be

February

Brugs Bierfestival (Bruges Beer Festival

3/2/2018 and 4/2/2018

For a whole weekend long, the courtyard of the Belfry, the City Halls, the Provincial Court and a tent on the Market Square are the places-to-beer, with a selection of some 400 top beers from 80 Belgian brewers. A delicious delight for your taste-buds!

INFO > www.brugsbierfestival.be

Bits of Dance

22/2/2018 – 25/2/2018

A new dance festival where young dancers, choreographers and performers from home and abroad can show what they are made of. Because young talent deserves a stage.

INFO > www.ccbrugge.be

March

Beaufort

30/3/2018 – 30/9/2018

For the sixth time, the three-yearly Beaufort event guarantees unexpected confrontations with the modern art of internationally respected artists at locations along the Belgian coast *(also see page 145)*.

INFO > www.beaufort18.be and www.dekust.be

April

More Music!

4/4/2018 – 8/4/2018

The Bruges Concert Hall and the Cactus Music Centre once again join forces to make More Music!, an exciting encounter between diverse and contrasting musical worlds. The result is an intriguing total concept that takes the visitor on an adventurous voyage of musical discovery.

INFO > www.moremusicfestival.be

MOOOV-filmfestival

18/4/2018 – 26/4/2018

MOOOV once again offers the very best films from around the world in Cinema Lumière. From Argentine thrillers to South Korean humour: discover it all in the heart of Bruges city centre!

INFO > www.mooov.be

Meifoor (May Fair)

20/4/2018 – 13/5/2018

For three fun-filled weeks some 90 fairground attractions 'take over' 't Zand, the Beursplein, the Koning Albertpark and the Simon Stevinplein.

'14-'18, the battle for the North Sea

21/4/2018 – 31/8/2018

Exhibition in the Provincial Court *(also see page 130)*

A CENTURIES OLD PROCESSION
10/5/2018

Each year on Ascension Day, the Holy Blood Procession takes place in Bruges in front of huge
crowds. To begin with, members of the clergy,
the brotherhoods and various costumed groups
play out scenes from the Bible. This is followed
by the story of the relic of the Holy Blood. In 1146,
during the Second Crusade, Count Thierry of Al-
sace was able to obtain a few drops of the blood
of Christ from the Patriarch of Jerusalem. This
precious relic was brought to Bruges in 1150,

where it has been venerated ever since in the Basilica of the Holy Blood.

May

Budapest Festival
16/5/2018 – 19/5/2018

A music festival with concerts by the
celebrated Budapest Festival Orchestra, conducted by Iván Fischer.
This year the music of Gustav Mahler is
central, a composer who transformed
simple German songs into tragic sym-
phonic creations.
INFO > www.concertgebouw.be

Airbag Festival
18/5/2018 – 3/6/2018

This biannual international accordion
festival is this year celebrating its
eighth edition. Accordion virtuoso Gwen
Cresens, the first guest curator, takes
you on a voyage of musical discovery,
often with adventurous combinations
and genres.
INFO > www.ccbrugge.be/airbag

June

Navy Days
30/6/2018 and 1/7/2018

In Zeebrugge, under the expert
supervision of Belgian and international sailors, you can hop from
one impressive ship to another.
With numerous small exhibitions
and demonstrations.
INFO > www.mil.be/navycomp

July

Zandfeesten (Zand Festival)
1/7/2018

Flanders' largest antiques and second-
hand market on 't Zand, the Beursplein
and in the Koning Albertpark attracts
bargain-hunters from far and wide.

Cactusfestival
13/7/2018 – 15/7/2018

An atmospheric open-air music festival in the Minnewater Park, with a
cocktail of contemporary music in all

its diversity. Internationally famous but with a warm and friendly family ambiance, liberally spiced with a wide selection of fringe activities and culinary offerings.

INFO > www.cactusfestival.be

MOODS!
27/7/2018 – 9/8/2018

Musical and other fireworks at unforgettable locations in Bruges city centre, such as the Belfry courtyard and the Burg. In unique settings, you will be able to enjoy top national and international acts at one of the evening concerts.

INFO > www.moodsbrugge.be

August

MAfestival
3/8/2018 – 12/8/2018

Each year this highly respected festival of Ancient Music – MA stands for Musica Antiqua – continues to attract the world's top performers to Bruges and Bruges' wood- and wetlands. In 2018, the MAfestival will turn the spotlight onto *Femmes Fatales*.

INFO > www.mafestival.be
(You can read more about Early Music in the interview with Albert Edelman on pages 120-123)

Zandfeesten (Zand Festival)
5/8/2018

Flanders' largest antiques and second-hand market on 't Zand, the Beursplein and in the Koning Albertpark.

GOLD BRUGGE
7/5/2018 – 13/5/2018

This new festival brings together many of the most attractive elements of Bruges' golden century: fascinating history, marvellous architecture, stunning art and, above all, the magic of Bruges' polyphonic music, which in its day was as renowned throughout Europe as the paintings of the Flemish primitives. Follow the story of the Bruges magistrate and alderman Donaas de Moor in the melodious tones of Jacob Obrechts' *Missa de Sancto Donationo*, the highlight of GOLD, performed in St. James's Church, where the piece was first composed some 500 years ago.

INFO > www.concertgebouw.be

Benenwerk (Leg-work) – Ballroom Brugeoise
11/8/2018

Put your best leg forward for a festival that is guaranteed to bring out the dancer in you. Spread across various locations in Bruges city centre, you will be swept along by live bands and DJs for a dance marathon at different ball-

MAGNIFICENT CATHEDRAL CONCERTS
April to September

For more than 60 years, many re-nowned organists, choirs and solo-ists from both home and abroad have given the best of themselves during the cathedral concerts in St. Saviour's Cathedral *(also see page 70-71)*. Amongst others, Marcel Dupré, one of the greatest organ virtuosos of the 20th century, once played on the cathedral's centuries' old organ. Cultural pleasure of the highest quality. Not to be missed.
INFO > www.kathedraalconcerten.be

rooms, offering the most divergent dance music.
INFO > www.benenwerk.be

Brugse Kantdagen (Bruges Lace Days)
16/8/2018 – 19/8/2018
Mid-August, the Walplein and the buildings of the Halve Maan Brewery buzz with lace activities: information and exposition stands, lace sale and demonstrations.
INFO > www.kantcentrum.eu

(You read more about lace and the Lace Centre on page 64)

Lichtfeest (Festival of Light)
17/8/2018 and 18/8/2018
Lissewege, the 'white polder village', once again wraps itself in a shroud of light and conviviality. As soon as evening falls, you can enjoy atmospher-ic music, video art, street theatre, fire and light installations, etc.
INFO > www.bruggeplus.be

September

Open Monumentendag (Open Monument Day)
8/9/2018 and 9/9/2018
During the second weekend of Septem-ber, Flanders organises the 30th edition of Open Monument Day, when it opens the doors of its many monuments to the general public.
INFO > www.bruggeomd.be

Zandfeesten (Zand Festival)
23/9/2018
Antiques and second-hand market on 't Zand, the Beursplein and in the Koning Albertpark.

Kookeet (Cook-Eat)
29/9/2018 – 1/10/2018
The eighth edition of Kookeet is organ-ized in a stylish tented village. During this culinary event, 31 top chefs from in and around Bruges and one guest chef serve gastronomic dishes at reasonable prices *(also see page 91)*.
INFO > www.kookeet.be

October

Iedereen klassiek (Everyone Classic)
27/10/2018

Classical music radio station Klara and the Concert Hall join forces to allow you to explore the beauty of Bach, Beethoven and Bruges. This festival is traditionally brought to a close with a performance by the Brussels Philharmonic Orchestra.
INFO > www.concertgebouw.be

November

Jazz Brugge Festival
16/11/2018 – 18/11/2018

This edition focuses on transnational, intercultural meetings. With artistic cross-fertilization between different continents and different generations, musical fireworks are guaranteed!
INFO > www.concertgebouw.be, www.kaap.be

December

Christmas Market and ice rink
23/11/2018 – 1/1/2019

For more than a month, you can immerse yourself in the true Christmas atmosphere on the Market Square and at the Simon Stevinplein; on the Market Square you can even pull on your ice skates.

CARILLON CONCERTS

Throughout the year, you can enjoy free, live carillon concerts in Bruges on Wednesdays, Saturdays and Sundays from 11.00 a.m. to 12.00 p.m. From mid-June to mid-September, evening concerts also take place on Mondays and Wednesdays from 9.00 p.m. to 10.00 p.m. The inner courtyard of the Belfry is a good place to listen.
INFO > www.carillon-brugge.be

December Dance
6/12/2018 – 16/12/2018

The annual rendezvous for dancelovers from all over the world. Over a number of days, this festival brings together established names and young talent at a range of unique locations in the city. The 2018 edition concentrates on dance from Australia and New Zealand.
INFO > www.decemberdance.be

All dates are subject to possible change.

Cultural temples

♿ 📶 17 Concertgebouw (Concert Hall)

This international music and art centre is a place that offers the very best in contemporary dance and classical music. The impressive Concert Auditorium (1,289 seats) and intimate Chamber Music Hall (322 seats) are famed for their excellent acoustics. In the Concert Hall, you can also admire various contemporary works of art. Also take a look behind the scenes by following the Concertgebouw Circuit *(see page 53)*.

INFO AND TICKETS > 't Zand 34, opening hours of the Concertgebouw Circuit or tel. +32 (0)70 22 33 02 (Monday to Friday, 4.30 p.m.-6.30 p.m.), www.concertgebouw.be

29 KAAP | De Werf

KAAP Creative Compass, the centre for contemporary art, supports creative talent in Bruges at two separate locations: De Werf and De Groenplaats. In De Groenplaats, young artists and performers can develop their work in peaceful and quiet surroundings. De Werf is the place for anyone who loves exciting theatre and swinging jazz from the four corners of the world. But KAAP also likes to go out onto the streets, filling the city's open spaces with public and performers. KAAP is your creative compass for Bruges.

INFO AND TICKETS > Werfstraat 108, tel. +32 (0)70 22 12 12 (Monday to Saturday, 10.00 a.m.-5.00 p.m. and Sunday and

Concert Hall

City Theatre

public holidays, 10.00 a.m-2.00 p.m.),
www.kaap.be

♿ 🛜 32 Magdalenazaal (MaZ, Magdalena Concert Hall)

Its 'black-box' architecture means that
the MaZ is the ideal location for all
kinds of events. The Bruges Cultural
Centre and the Cactus Music Festival
both organize pop and rock concerts
here. Major artists from the world
of music and more intimate club
talents can all 'do their own thing' in
the MaZ. Rising stars in the theatrical
and dance arts also perform in this
perfect setting. Children's and family
events are regular features on the
programme.

INFO AND TICKETS > Magdalena-
straat 27, Sint-Andries, tel. +32 (0)50
44 30 60 (Tuesday to Friday, 1.00 p.m.-

5.00 p.m. and Saturday, 4.00 p.m.-
7.00 p.m., closed 1/7 to 15/8),
www.ccbrugge.be

♿ 43 Stadsschouwburg (City Theatre)

The Bruges City Theatre (1869) is one of
the best-preserved theatres of its kind
in Europe and was fully restored in
2001. The sober neo-Renaissance facade of this royal theatre conceals a palatial foyer and an equally magnificent
auditorium. This outstanding infra-
structure is used for performances of
contemporary dance and theatre and
for concerts of various kinds.

INFO AND TICKETS > Vlamingstraat 29,
tel. +32 (0)50 44 30 60 (Tuesday to Friday, 1.00 p.m.-5.00 p.m. and Saturday
4.00 p.m.-7.00 p.m., closed 1/7 to 15/8),
www.ccbrugge.be

Shopping in Bruges

Steenstraat

Bruges has lots of shops to offer you something special: authentic places that surprise you again and again with their clever and original products. The city is rightly famous for its harmonious mix of creative and trendy newcomers, vintage addresses where nostalgia rules, and classic establishments that have been run with success for decades by the same family.

HANDMADE IN BRUGES:
A CITY OF INSPIRED CRAFTSMEN (AND WOMEN)

Bruges is often associated with the skill and virtuosity of its master craftsmen from the Middle Ages, but today the city is still home to creative craftsmanship of many kinds. You will be pleasantly surprised by the number of craft addresses throughout the city. The Handmade in Bruges city plan (available free of charge in Dutch, French and English in the ℹ️ info-offices) puts today's craftsmen and women quite literally on the map. In the Handmade shops you can find lots of fun presents for yourself or to take back home for family and friends.

Perhaps some calligraphy or engraved stonework, or maybe a handmade skate-board or some modern lingerie in traditional Bruges lace? Or what about something tasty from one of the many traditional-style food and drink stores? From beer and chocolate, through colourful sweets and oven-fresh biscuits, to deliciously baked bread and cakes: you can find it all in Bruges! And don't forget to pop into De Makersrepubliek at Sint-Jakobsstraat 33, where you can find regular exhibitions and creative pop-up stores, as well as workshops and lectures. Discover more about the affiliated craftsmen/women and their inspiring stories on www.handmadeinbrugge.be.

Where to shop?

Because Bruges is pedestrian-friendly
and the main streets are all close to each
other, a day's shopping here is a relaxing
experience. You will find all the major national and international chains, as well as
trendy local boutiques and plenty of interesting new discoveries. The most important shopping streets (indicated in yellow
on the removable city map) run between
the Market Square and the old city gates:
Steenstraat, Simon Stevinplein, Mariastraat, Zuidzandstraat, Sint-Jakobsstraat, Sint-Amandsstraat, Geldmuntstraat, Noordzandstraat, Smedenstraat,
Vlamingstraat, Academiestraat, Philipstockstraat, Hoogstraat, Langestraat and
Katelijnestraat. There is also a small but
elegant shopping centre, the Zilverpand,
between Noordzandstraat and Zuidzandstraat. Each neighbourhood has its own
unique atmosphere. In Steenstraat, for
example, you will find the famous brand
names, whereas Langestraat boasts
many little second-hand and bric-à-brac
shops. The large hypermarkets are located just outside the city centre.
Spoilt for choice? On www.visitbruges.
be you can find a selection of the very
best shopping addresses in Bruges city
centre: a mix of authentic shops offering products made in Bruges and renowned specialist stores that have
concentrated with success on a single
product (line) for more than 25 years.
You can find more fun shopping tips in the
chapter 'Tips from Bruges experts', pages
102-103, 110-111, 118-119, 126-127, 134-135.

When to shop?

Most shops operate from Monday to Saturday, opening at 10.00 a.m. and closing
at either 6.00 or 6.30 p.m. Many specialist stores are open on Sunday as well.
And on 'Shopping Sundays' – the first
Sunday of the month, except on public
holidays, from 1.00 p.m. to 6.00 p.m. –
they are joined by many of the other
shops. To make your shopping experience more pleasant, there is restricted
access for traffic on Saturday afternoon
and 'Shopping Sundays' (from 1.00 p.m.
to 6.00 p.m.) in the following shopping
streets: Zuidzandstraat, Steenstraat,
Geldmuntstraat and Noordzandstraat.

Typical Bruges souvenirs

Bruges was a flourishing centre of the
diamond trade as early as the 14th century, and the city also boasted several pro-
fessional diamond-cutting establishments. In the diamond laboratory of the
Bruges Diamond Museum, you will learn
how all that sparkling splendour is as-
sessed and processed. After that, it's
only a matter of checking out the museum shop or the many other jewellery
stores in the city with a keen connois-

seur's eye before making your move – and cashing in. *You can find more information about the Bruges Diamond Museum on pages 60-61.*

Since time immemorial, lace has also been inextricably connected to Bruges. Once upon a time, as many as a quarter of all the women in the city were employed making lace. Nowadays, you can still see female lace-makers in action in several of the Bruges lace shops. *You can find more information about lace and the Lace Centre on page 64.*

The people of Bruges have always liked a glass or two of good beer. The city boasts several excellent locally made ales – *Straffe Hendrik* and *Brugse Zot*, both brewed by De Halve Maan Brewery, right

in the heart of the historic city centre – as well as eight traditional-style beers, including the *Fort Lapin 8 Triple* and the *Fort Lapin 10 Quadruple*, both brewed in the Fort Lapin Brewery on the edge of the city, and the *Bourgogne des Flanders*, which you can sample in the brewery of the same name along the Dijver. Have we convinced you? Then why not visit the annual Bruges Beer Festival or the Bruges Beer Experience on the Markt. *You can find more information about the Halve Maan and Bourgogne des Flandres breweries and the Bruges Beer Experience on pages 57-59; more information about the Bruges Beer Festival on page 79.*

Perhaps you are not such a fan of beer? Those with a sweet tooth can visit one of more than 50 chocolate boutiques that cater to all tastes: from deliciously old-fashioned chocolate blocks, through finger-licking good pralines that melt in your mouth, to ingenious molecular chocolate preparations tailored to the requirements of the city's star chefs. *Read more about chocolate on page 59-60.*

Brugsch Swaentje

Gastronomic Bruges

With its impressive number of top-quality restaurants, Bruges is a paradise for gastronomes. The range of culinary excellence on offer varies from Michelin-star cooking to stylish local brasseries serving good and honest (inter)national specialities.

KOOKEET - A MAJOR CULINARY FESTIVAL, WITH TOP BRUGES CHEFS AND A GUEST CHEF

Each year, more than 100,000 people visit the Kookeet culinary festival, which this year celebrates its eighth edition. The recipe for success? For three days, top Bruges chefs and one guest chef serve up gastronomic gems at democratic prices. The visitors can put together their own menus at their own pace. The participating Bruges chefs are all top names in their field and have one or more Michelin stars, a mention in Bib Gourmand or a high score in Gault&Millau.

You can find more info on page 82 and on www.kookeet.be.

Award winning restaurants

» **De Jonkman**   Maalse Steenweg 438, 8310 Sint-Kruis, tel. +32 (0)50 36 07 67, www.dejonkman.be (2 Michelin-stars, 18/20 graded by Gault&Millau)

» **Zet'Joe**   Langestraat 11, 8000 Brugge, tel. +32 (0)50 33 82 59, www.zetjoe.be (1 Michelin-star, 17/20 graded by Gault&Millau)

» **Sans Cravate**   Langestraat 159, 8000 Brugge, tel. +32 (0)50 67 83 10, www.sanscravate.be (1 Michelin-star, 16.5/20 graded by Gault&Millau)

» **Den Gouden Harynck**   Groeninge 25, 8000 Brugge, tel. +32 (0)50 33 76 37, www.goudenharynck.be (1 Michelin-star, 16/20 graded by Gault&Millau)

» **Auberge De Herborist**   De Watermolen 15, 8200 Sint-Andries, tel. +32 (0)50 38 76 00, www.aubergedeherborist.be (1 Michelin-star, 15/20 graded by Gault&Millau)

» **Goffin**   Maalse Steenweg 2, 8310 Sint-Kruis, tel. +32 (0)50 68 77 88, www.timothygoffin.be (1 Michelin-star, 15/20 graded by Gault&Millau)

» **Bistro Bruut**   Meestraat 9, 8000 Brugge, tel. +32 (0)50 69 55 09, www.bistrobruut.be (15.5/20 graded by Gault&Millau, winner of the Gastro-Bistro of the Year Award)

» **L.E.S.S.**   Torhoutse Steenweg 479, 8200 Sint-Michiels, tel. +32 (0)50 69 93 69, www.l-e-s-s.be (15/20 graded by Gault&Millau)

» **Patrick Devos**   Zilverstraat 41, 8000 Brugge, tel. +32 (0)50 33 55 66, www.patrickdevos.be (15/20 graded by Gault&Millau)

» **Rock-Fort**   Langestraat 15-17, 8000 Brugge, tel. +32 (0)50 33 41 13, www.rock-fort.be (15/20 graded by Gault&Millau)

» **Bistro Refter**   Molenmeers 2, 8000 Brugge, tel. +32 (0)50 44 49 00, www.bistrorefter.be (14/20 graded by Gault&Millau and selected as a Bib Gourmand)

» **bonte B**   Dweersstraat 12, 8000 Brugge, tel. +32 (0)50 34 83 43, www.restaurantbonteb.be (14/20 graded by Gault&Millau)

» **Floris**   Gistelse Steenweg 520, 8200 Sint-Andries, tel. +32 (0)50 73 60 20, www.florisrestaurant.be (14/20 graded by Gault&Millau)

» **Hubert Gastrobar**   Langestraat 159, 8000 Brugge, tel. +32 (0)50 64 10 09, www.gastrobar-hubert.be (14/20 graded by Gault&Millau)

» **Le Mystique**   Niklaas Desparsstraat 11, 8000 Brugge, tel. +32 (0)50 44 44 45, www.lemystique.be (14/20 graded by Gault&Millau)

» **'t Pandreitje**   Pandreitje 6, 8000 Brugge, tel. +32 (0)50 33 11 90, www.pandreitje.be (14/20 graded by Gault&Millau)

» **Tanuki**   Oude Gentweg 1, 8000 Brugge, tel. +32 (0)50 34 75 12, www.tanuki.be (14/20 graded by Gault&Millau)

» **Tête Pressée**   Koningin Astridlaan 100, 8200 Sint-Michiels, tel. +32 (0)470 21 26 27, www.tetepressee.be (14/20 graded by Gault&Millau)

» **Assiette Blanche**   Philipstockstraat 23-25, 8000 Brugge, tel. +32 (0)50 34 00 94, www.assietteblanche.be (13/20 graded by Gault&Millau and selected as a Bib Gourmand)

» **De Mangerie**   Oude Burg 20, 8000 Brugge, tel. +32 (0)50 33 93 36, www.mangerie.com (13/20 graded by Gault&Millau)

- » **Franco Belge**   Langestraat 109, 8000 Brugge, tel. +32 (0)50 69 56 48,
  www.restaurantfrancobelge.be (13/20 graded by Gault&Millau)
- » **Kok au Vin**   Ezelstraat 21, 8000 Brugge, tel. +32 (0)50 33 95 21,
  www.kok-au-vin.be (13/20 graded by Gault&Millau and selected as a Bib Gourmand)
- » **La Tâche**   Blankenbergse Steenweg 1, 8000 Sint-Pieters, tel. +32 (0)50 68 02 52,
  www.latache.be (13/20 graded by Gault&Millau)
- » **Lieven**   Philipstockstraat 45, 8000 Brugge, tel. +32 (0)50 68 09 75,
  www.etenbijlieven.be (13/20 graded by Gault&Millau)
- » **'t Zwaantje**   Gentpoortvest 70, 8000 Brugge, tel. +32 (0)473 71 25 80,
  www.hetzwaantje.be (13/20 graded by Gault&Millau)
- » **Bhavani**   Simon Stevinplein 5, 8000 Brugge, tel. +32 (0)50 33 90 25,
  www.bhavani.be (12/20 graded by Gault&Millau)
- » **Bistro Rombaux**   Moerkerkse Steenweg 139, 8310 Sint-Kruis,
  tel. +32 (0)50 73 79 49, www.bistrorombaux.be (12/20 graded by Gault&Millau)
- » **Cantine Copine**   Steenkaai 34, 8000 Brugge, tel. +32 (0)470 97 04 55,
  www.cantinecopine.be (12/20 graded by Gault&Millau)
- » **De Florentijnen**   Academiestraat 1, 8000 Brugge, tel. +32 (0)50 67 75 33,
  www.deflorentijnen.be (12/20 graded by Gault&Millau)
- » **De Visscherie**   Vismarkt 8, 8000 Brugge, tel. +32 (0)50 33 02 12,
  www.visscherie.be (12/20 graded by Gault&Millau)
- » **Duc de Bourgogne**   Huidenvettersplein 12, 8000 Brugge, tel. +32 (0)50 33 20 38,
  www.ducdebourgogne.be (12/20 graded by Gault&Millau)
- » **Huyze Die Maene**   Markt 17, 8000 Brugge, tel. +32 (0)50 33 39 59,
  www.huyzediemaene.be (12/20 graded by Gault&Millau)
- » **'t Jong Gerecht**   Langestraat 119, 8000 Brugge, tel. +32 (0)50 31 32 32,
  www.tjonggerecht.be (12/20 graded by Gault&Millau)
- » **Kwizien Divien**   Hallestraat 4, 8000 Brugge, tel. +32 (0)50 34 71 29,
  www.kwiziendivien.be (12/20 graded by Gault&Millau)
- » **La Buena Vista**   Sint-Clarastraat 43, 8000 Brugge, tel. +32 (0)50 33 38 96
  (12/20 graded by Gault&Millau)
- » **Parkrestaurant**   Minderbroedersstraat 1, 8000 Brugge, tel. +32 (0)497 80 18 72,
  www.parkrestaurant.be (12/20 graded by Gault&Millau)
- » **The Blue Lobster**   Tijdokstraat 9, 8380 Zeebrugge, tel. +32 (0)50 68 45 71,
  www.thebluelobster.be (12/20 graded by Gault&Millau)
- » **'t Werftje**   Werfkaai 29, 8380 Zeebrugge, tel. +32 (0)497 55 30 10,
  www.twerftje.be (12/20 graded by Gault&Millau)
- » **Tou.Gou**   Smedenstraat 47, 8000 Brugge, tel. +32 (0)50 70 58 02,
  www.tougou.be (selected as a Bib Gourmand)

More tips on finding the right address for you can be found in the section
'Tips from Bruges experts', pages 100-101, 108-109, 116-117, 124-125, 132-133.

Huidenvettersplein

Tips from
Bruges
experts

Bruges: World Heritage city

Sonia Papili reveals
the Italian side of Bruges

Rozenhoedkaai

During the week, Italian Sonia Papili studies the North Sea with academic sobriety; during the weekend, she guides her fellow countrymen with great passion around her adopted city. A passion that began gradually some twelve years ago, but now burns more brightly than ever.

ID-CARD

Name: Sonia Papili
Nationality: Italian
Date of birth: 17 May 1972
Has lived in Bruges since 2006. Sonia is a geologist with the Ministry of Defence and a tourist guide in Bruges.

Two geologists – him attached to the University of Ghent, her attached to the University of Rome – who met on a ship in Istanbul to discuss climate change: there are worse ways to start a long-distance relationship. For three years, the pair commuted back and forth between Italy and Belgium before finally deciding to settle in Bruges. 'I had only been in Bruges once before,' says Sonia. 'I was much more familiar with Ghent, but my husband thought that Bruges better suited my personality and temperament. And he was right: Bruges really is my city!' In the meantime, Sonia learnt Dutch and started work here as a geologist. During her citizenship programme, she became more and more curious about the history of her new home town. 'During the language course they told us a little bit about the history of the place. This intrigued me and so I decided to take a three-year course to become an official guide in Bruges.'

'I was much more familiar with Ghent, but my husband thought that Bruges better suited my personality and temperament. And he was right: Bruges really is my city!'

WHY BRUGES IS A WORLD HERITAGE CITY

In 1998, the Bruges Beguinage was recognized as a World Heritage site. A year later, the Belfry received similar recognition. In 2000, this was extended to cover the entire city centre. Since 2009, the Holy Blood Procession has been listed as an item of immaterial World Heritage. Bruges also has a valuable and impressive architectural patrimony and is a fine example of an architecturally harmonious city. In particular, Bruges is famed for its Gothic style buildings in brick. In addition, its authentic and organically developed medieval urban fabric has been perfectly preserved and it is also the 'birthplace' of the Flemish primitives. In other words, reasons enough for UNESCO to label Bruges as a 'World Heritage city'.

XPLORE BRUGES – The official city tour app of Bruges

You can discover all the secrets of Bruges with the free Xplore Bruges-app. There are city walks, cycling circuits and indoor trails. Almost all the routes are available in five languages: English, Dutch, French, German and Spanish. At the moment, there are eleven different routes: from 'Bruges, anno 1562', through 'The hidden treasures of St. James's Church', to 'Handmade in Bruges'. In short, something for everyone!

Tip: download the app at home or from any wifi network, you no longer need access to mobile internet. If you are not familiar with downloading apps, check out the routes on the website www. xplorebruges.be.

Italian art

During her guide training, Sonia soon discovered that she was not the first Italian to lose her heart to Bruges. From the 13th to the 15th century, Bruges was an international trading centre that had close links with Europe's other great trading cities. This also meant with the great Italian cities, who around 1300 had decided to focus on international trade by sea as the best way to achieve fame and fortune, and saw Bruges as an ideal base for their activities in Northern Europe. Inspired by the success of the Italian merchants, the traders of other countries soon found their way to Bruges, which rapidly grew to become a northern counterpart to Venice. And so the 'Venice of the North' was born. 'A fine discovery for me, and one which made me look at the city – and in particular its Italian quarter – in a new light.'

'It is now widely known that the Italians traded here,' says Sonia, 'but they also left behind traces of their artistic heritage.' Sonia's thesis for her guide's training course dealt with the works of Italian art that can still be found in

Bruges. 'Of course, there is the *Madonna and Child* by Michelangelo in the Church of Our Lady, but there are many other Italian masterpieces to admire as well. I am thinking of the poetic *Veins of the Convent* by Giuseppe Penone in the Old St. John site. Or the three works by the contemporary artist Mario Molinari, who is famous in Italy, one of which is in the Kustlaan in Zeebrugge, near the old fish auction site. I also suspect that the beautiful medallions of Lorenzo de' Medici and his wife Clarice Orsini in the Bladelin Court were made in Italy, but I have found no evidence for this so far.'

'What is beyond doubt is the fact that de' Medici, a family of 15th century Florentine bankers, did once run a bank from the Bladelin Court. I am also very impressed by the most recent statues on the facade of the City Hall. These were carved in the 1980s by Stefaan Depuydt (1937-2016) and his Italian wife, Livia Canestraro. Two of the statues are self-portraits of the couple. In fact, there are lots of places in Bruges where you can discover their work. They are a testimony to how beautiful and successful artistic collaboration between differing nationalities can sometimes be.'

Starting young

Nowadays, Sonia passes on her love for Bruges to her former compatriots. 'Of course, the Italians love it when they are guided around the city in their own language. It is very often their first visit to Bruges, and because I understand them perhaps a little bit better than other guides, I can also show them a little bit more of the things that really interest them. Naturally, they first want to know what it's like to live here, about the schools and the medical system, about people's attitudes to work and leisure... With my hand on my heart, I can assure them that life here is really good.'

In the meantime, Sonia's own family also know where to find all the best places in Bruges. 'The city continues to evolve. As soon as anything new appears, I immediately want to check it out. In this way, my three daughters also get to share in my love of Bruges from an early age!'

If you want to discover the beauty of Bruges with an official guide, please turn to page 49.

Veins of the Convent

Sonia Papili
Best addresses

FAVOURITE SPOT

» **Coupure**

'I am a big fan of the **Coupure**, a spot in the middle of the city but a million miles away from all the hustle and bustle. The way in which the majestic rows of trees draw a green line along Coupure canal is pure art. What's more, our family is linked to the Coupure in a very special way. During the Bruges Triennial 2018 a floating platform with a pop-up bar will be set up on the canal.'

RESTAURANTS

» **La Tâche**, Blankenbergse Steenweg 1, tel. +32 (0)50 68 02 52, www.latache.be

'My husband went to eat here a few times and was always full of praise for the food. The restaurant – housed in a beautiful city mansion – is known for its classic cooking laced with the flavours of the South. That's why La Tâche is at the top of my 'must visit' list.'

» **Sans Cravate**, Langestraat 159, tel. +32 (0)50 67 83 10, www.sanscravate.be

'Our absolute favourite. Sans Cravate now has a star - and fully deserved. It's not somewhere we go every month, but if we have something special to celebrate, then we like to do it here! Chef Henk prepares both classic and contemporary dishes.'

» De Schaar, Hooistraat 2, tel. +32 (0)50 33 59 79, www.bistrodeschaar.be
'This is the perfect place for anyone who wants to enjoy to the full the Coupure - my favourite place in the city. In the summer, it's wonderful to just sit on a terrace at the water's edge; in the winter, you can enjoy the lovely open fire inside.'

» De Bottelier, Sint-Jakobsstraat 63, tel. +32 (0)50 33 18 60,
www.debottelier.com
'This is a real no-nonsense address with healthy cooking focused mainly on vegetables. And reasonably priced as well! Add to this a charming interior and you will soon understand why the sign 'full' often hangs in the window.'

» Du Phare, Sasplein 2, tel. +32 (0)50 34 35 90, www.duphare.be
'After a pleasant summer walk along the ramparts or a climb up one of the windmill hills, there is nothing nicer than getting your breath back on the large sun terrace of Du Phare. And if the weather is not kind, you can enjoy the elegant interior of this top-class bistro with its seasonal, international cuisine.'

CAFÉS

» De Belleman Pub, Jozef Suvée-straat 22, tel. +32 (0)50 34 19 89
'Local people affectionately call this traditional brown café on the corner of the Koningin Astridpark 'The Belleman's'. I love the classic British pub-atmosphere and the fact that you can chat to locals who have sat at the same place at the bar for years and years.'

» De Proeverie, Katelijnestraat 6, tel. +32 (0)50 33 08 87,
www.deproeverie.be
'The best hot chocolate in Bruges comes from this British-style tearoom. Freshly melted chocolate with warm milk: what more can you want? Perhaps something from their delicious selection of homemade ice-creams, cupcakes and scones! A visit to De Proeverie is always lip-licking good!'

» **Café Rose Red**, Cordoeaniersstraat 16, tel. +32 (0)50 33 90 51,
www.caferosered.com

'To be honest, I am not a big drinker, more a sipper and a taster. And there is no better place to do this than in Café Rose Red, with its fine range of the very best Belgian beers. They have dozens of them!'

» **De Zolder**, Vlamingstraat 53, tel. +32 (0)477 24 49 05

'A cellar cafe named 'De Zolder', which means 'attic' in Dutch: it could only happen in Belgium! De Zolder is a cool and relaxing café, where you can sample local beers in wonderful medieval surroundings. Ideal for a night-out with a group of friends.'

» **Grand Hotel Casselbergh**, Hoogstraat 6, tel. +32 (0)50 44 65 00,
www.grandhotelcasselbergh.com

'The elegant bar of the Grand Hotel Casselbergh is a great place to chill out before or after your evening dinner. You can sit at the bar counter or lounge in one of the deliciously comfortable easy chairs. This is the place to start or round off your evening on the town in style. People not staying at the hotel are always more than welcome.'

SHOPPING LIST

» **Callebert**, Wollestraat 25,
tel. +32 (0)50 33 50 61,
www.callebert.be

'As a design freak, I can always find something to set my pulse racing at Callebert, a style oasis where timeless beauty reigns supreme. Complete with a children's department that will tempt the adults as well!'

» **Da Vinci**, Geldmuntstraat 34, tel. +32 (0)50 33 36 50, www.davinci-brugge.be

'It doesn't matter if the weather is freezing cold or boiling hot: there are always tourists lined up in droves outside this deluxe ice-cream parlour. The number of different flavours is almost beyond belief. What's more, everything – from the ice-cream right down to the sauces – is made on the premises.'

» Krokodil, Sint-Jakobsstraat 47, tel. +32 (0)50 33 75 79, www.krokodil.be

'A regular port-of-call for people with kids. This not the place for 'throwaway' junk, but for beautiful and solidly made toys that will stand the test of time.'

» De Witte Pelikaan, Vlamingstraat 23, tel. +32 (0)50 34 82 84, www.dewittepelikaan.be

'Whoever loves Christmas will love De Witte Pelikaan, with its year-round selection of Christmas baubles and jingle bells.'

» BbyB, Sint-Amandsstraat 39, tel. +32 (0)50 70 57 60, www.bbyb.be

'At BbyB you can find a range of elegantly sleek haute couture chocolates that are almost impossible to resist. Time after time I am tempted by this classy concept store to try out new and exciting flavour combinations. Because let's admit it: who can say 'no' to chocolate with rhubarb, speculoos biscuit, 'babulettes' or star aniseed?'

SECRET TIP

» The remains of the old St. Donatian Cathedral, Burg 10, tel. +32 (0)50 44 68 44

'Under the prestigious Crowne Plaza Hotel lay hidden the remains of the **St. Donatian Cathedral**, which during the Middle Ages represented the ecclesiastical power of the Church on the Burg square. St. Donatian's was the court church of the counts of Flanders. If you really want to dig into the oldest parts of the city's historic past, ask at the reception desk if you can take a look in their cellar. Because in Bruges, the ground is always full of history.'

Modern art in a medieval city

Co-curator Michel Dewilde talks about 'his' Triennial

Tadashi Kawamata
Tree Huts in Bruges - Triennial 2015

In 2018, the Triennial will take over the heart of Bruges city centre for a second time, with the same gay abandon, passion and tongue-in-cheek contrariness as three years ago. Whoever looks at the Triennial's thought-provoking exhibits will see Bruges through different eyes. Co-curator Michel Dewilde about the pioneering role played by the city: 'World Heritage city, home of the Flemish primitives and … centre of contemporary art. It's hard to pigeon-hole Bruges in a single category.'

ID-CARD

Name: Michel Dewilde
Nationality: Belgian
Date of birth: 31 July 1963
Lives in Ghent. Michel Dewilde is responsible for the Visual Arts programme at the Cultuurcentrum (Cultural Centre) and is together with Till-Holger Borchert *(also see page 112-115)* curator of the 2018 Triennial, which returns to Bruges this year.

As an art expert and historian, Michel Dewilde worked professionally in almost all the great Flemish art towns before he finally arrived in Bruges. A city that everyone immediately associates with its world heritage status and the Flemish primitives, but is less well-known for its love and support for modern art.

'An unfortunate misunderstanding,' says the co-curator of the Bruges Triennial. 'When it comes to modern art, Bruges has a long history. Few people seem to remember it today, but in the 1960s the city played a pioneering role and occupied a prominent position on the national artistic map.' The oil crisis heralded in a period of 'hibernation', but Bruges is now once again demanding with confidence a leading position in the contemporary artistic scene. 'The continuity of that history was interrupted, a few links in the chain were broken, but we are now putting that right. There is a fresh new wind blowing through the city. More than that, Bruges is currently the only Belgian city with a Triennial.'

Top event with an international allure

Michel was one of the original initiators of the Bruges Triennial and so helped to start, along with his colleagues and the many visitors, a new chapter in the city's history. A huge leap forwards, which was an immediate hit with the public, right from the first edition in 2015. 'The first Triennial attracted local and national visitors, but also people who were just passing by and found it fun to see all the open spaces in the historic city centre packed with modern art and architecture. The second edition, in 2018, has set its ambitions even higher: this time we also want to attract international art lovers.'

An artistic route through the heart of the city

The event once again brings together an international selection of inspirational and celebrated artists and architects, whose installations, videos, images and other media form a route through the city. It's a roller-coaster of a ride, which constantly thrills and surprises with its interesting juxtapositions and daring

> 'Even people who think they have nothing to do with art
> pick up something as they wander through the city, so that they
> see Bruges in a slightly different and more artistic light.'

confrontations. Why daring? Because all these contemporary, ground-breaking and thought-provoking works are displayed in medieval settings of great historical beauty.

The unique field of tension this creates is what makes the Triennial so special. Michel Dewilde: 'You don't often find art in open spaces. Even when the Biennial descends on Venice, you hardly notice it around the city. All the art is carefully hidden away. Our approach is different. Bruges is much more than just a decor. The Triennial takes the city as its starting point and in this way it brings together visitors, companies, schools and local people. We want to be an added value, a motor for urban renewal.'

Art for everyone

The deliberately open approach of the Triennial creates a low threshold.

'Even people who have nothing to do with art, or think they have nothing to do with it, pick up something as they wander through the city, so that they see Bruges in a slightly different and more artistic light. For example, for the 2015 edition Atelier Bow-Wow installed a floating lounge on one of the canals. A multifunctional platform bobbing up and down in the heart of the city. I passed several times a day and always saw something different. In the morning, it was the older people who came, out for a walk by the water. At lunchtime, it was the students, enjoying a picnic lunch. In the afternoon, it was the swimmers and the party people. Each of them appropriated the platform for their own interests and purposes – and that's the way it should be.' Not surprisingly, this same successful approach is going to be repeat-

BRUGES TRIENNIAL 2018 | LIQUID CITY
5/5/2018 to 16/9/2018, A route through the historic centre of Bruges

The second edition of the Triennial looks at the fluid and continually changing nature of our society. *Liquid City* shows Bruges not only as a city quite literally surrounded by water, but also figuratively as a city that wants to function as a motor in the never-ending tide of social, cultural and political change. A place of diversity where people meet, but also a breeding ground for innovation and renewal.
Read more about the 2018 Triennial and check out some of the artworks on page 76-77, or else surf to www.triennalebrugge.be for all the info you need. Turn to pages 112-115 if you would like to read the interview with co-curator Till-Holger Borchert.

GALLERY-HOPPING WITH MICHEL DEWILDE

There are lots of galleries in Bruges. You can discover most of them by just wandering through the city, but others are more hidden. In Genthof, Michel likes to pop in at Gallery 44 ('a small but exquisite art temple dedicated to con-

temporary photography') and Gallery Pinsart ('an 18th century property that has been transformed into a space for modern art'). In Wollestraat, Michel always finds something to pleasantly surprise him in Art O Nivo ('a well-hidden and delightful oasis of art, packed with glass creations, ceramics, design and graphics'). You can find an overview of all the galleries in Bruges on www.visitbruges.be.

ed in the new 2018 Triennial, with a similar platform of the Coupure canal, in combination with the equally popular pop-up bar URB EGG.

Great expectations

The artists who take part in the Triennial are pleasantly surprised at the artistic freedom they are given in a World Heritage city. 'Am I really allowed to do

that?' is one of the most frequently asked questions I hear. And if I confirm, you can see how their creative ideas are quickly taken to the next level. It's a privilege for me to watch it happen.' For the 2018 edition, Michel Dewilde is expecting great things from the Argentine artist Tomás Saraceno. 'I am also looking forward to what the Americans, Africans and the Iranian Monir Shahroudy Farmanfarmaian are going to produce.' Once all the deadlines have been met and all the works are in place, Michel can breathe a huge sigh of relief when he cycles through the city. 'I think you can compare it with giving birth. First, there is absolute joy that you have been able to bring a wonderful son or daughter into the world. And then there is the equally wonderful knowledge that the rest of that world is going to come and visit you in the maternity ward!'

Michel Dewilde
Best addresses

FAVOURITE SPOT

» Smedenpoort

'From the **Smedenpoort** city gate you can still admire the medieval structure of the Bruges ramparts. You can clearly see the double earth wall and the double moats. Walk across the prize-winning footbridges and note the bronze skull, a gruesome reminder of a 17th-century traitor who wanted to let a hostile French army into the city through this gate.'

RESTAURANTS

» Lieven, Philipstockstraat 45, tel. +32 (0)50 68 09 75, www.etenbijlieven.be

'Honest and pure cooking with day-fresh products and a menu that offers the best of every season, all enjoyed in a stylish setting. That's Lieven in a nutshell.'

» Assiette Blanche, Philipstockstraat 23-25, tel. +32 (0)50 34 00 94, www.assietteblanche.be

'Lieven's neighbour, Assiette Blanche, serves classic French and Belgian dishes as well as favourite local specialities. I am thinking in particular of the buttermilk mashed potato with hand-peeled grey shrimps and a poached farmyard egg, or else the fillet of West Flanders Red beef.'

» Bocca, Dweersstraat 13, tel. +32 (0)50 61 61 75, www.bocca.be

'A great address for a quick and affordable lunch. Homemade pasta, sandwiches and salads that you can put together yourself.'

» NooN, Hoogstraat 32, tel. +32 (0)50 33 13 55, www.the-noon.com
'NooN, the revamped version of Restaurant Ryad, is a place where the message is clearly 'sharing is caring'. Useful to know: NooN has a selection of vegetarian, lactose-free and gluten-free dishes.'

» Exki, Stationsplein 5, tel. +32 (0)50 38 83 43, www.exki.be
'If you are looking for something healthy to take with you on the train or want a tasty bite to eat before you go, Exki is the place for you. Seasonal and regional vegetable products are the order of the day.'

CAFÉS

» Café Vlissinghe, Blekersstraat 2, tel. +32 (0)50 34 37 37, www.cafevlissinghe.be
'I enjoy dropping in to the oldest - but still very much thriving - café in town. Even though Café Vlissinghe is more than 500 years old, its popularity

means you sometimes have to fight for a place. A regular haunt for locals, a pleasant discovery for chance passers-by.'

» Stoepa, Oostmeers 124, tel. +32 (0)50 33 04 54, www.stoepa.be
'World cooking in a world interior. Once you're in the walled garden, you could easily imagine yourself to be a thousand kilometres further south. A place where the sun shines just a little more brightly.'

» URB EGG pop-upbar 2018, Coupure, www.triennalebrugge.be
'Since 2015, URB EGG has been the trendy place-to-be, where tourists and local people meet. This year, the temporary bar will set up shop on the Coupure canal. Away from the hustle and bustle of the city centre, it's a great place to relax and reflect on the Triennial whilst sipping a glass of something pleasant.'

» Books & Brunch, Garenmarkt 30, tel. +32 (0)50 70 90 79, www.booksandbrunch.be
'If you want to combine excellent breakfasts, brunches and lunches with picking up a second-hand book or two, Books & Brunch will be right up your street. The kind of place where you buy more than you ever intended.'

» Het Visioen, Katelijnestraat 160, tel. +32 (0)50 73 40 06, www.hetvisioen.com
'This brasserie reminds me of a Paris bistro. It has a pleasant terrace looking out over the water and serves Belgian-French cuisine with an Asian twist. A place where two worlds meet.'

SHOPPING LIST

» Boekhandel Raaklijn,
Kuipersstraat 1, tel. +32 (0)50 33 67 20, www.raaklijn.be
'You can always find plenty of book fanatics in this Bruges book temple. Here there are no annoying beats, just a delicious silence and carefully considered personal recommendations so that you can choose your books in peace.'

» Jüttu, Noordzandstraat 54, tel. +32 (0)50 33 10 06, www.juttu.be
'This concept store specializes in timeless fashion for him and her. You can also find some unusual articles for your interior and a selection of original beauty and food items. The tempting mix of strong international brands and local initiatives works well.'

» Bakkerij Sint-Paulus, Vlamingstraat 25, tel. +32 (0)50 34 85 70,
www.bakkerij-sint-paulus.be
'This Bruges bakery has been going for 50 years and treats you every day to forty different kinds of bread and a delicious selection of cakes, pastries and other confectionary. Mouth-wateringly good.'

» **Patisserie Schaeverbeke**, Schaarstraat 2, tel. +32 (0)50 33 31 82, www.schaeverbeke.be

'If you want to try some of their delicious goodies, ranging from butter buns and ten-grain bread to their marvellous chocolate pear cake, you will probably have to queue up like the rest of us. But whatever you buy, it will be well worth the wait.'

» **Depot d'O**, Riddersstraat 1, tel. +32 (0)495 23 65 95, www.depotdo.be

'A shop where you can pick up both vintage design and curiosities (I recently saw a lion's head and a life-sized stuffed zebra!). This eclectic mix makes Depot d'O truly irresistible.'

SECRET TIP

» **The Poertoren (Gunpowder tower) and garden**, Begijnenvest

'Close to the Minnewater bridge stands the solid bulk of the **Gunpowder tower**. Built in 1397 as a defensive tower, it was converted into a powder magazine about a century later. Today at its foot, often unnoticed by passers-by, there is a romantic vegetable garden and orchard. Fruit trees blossom between the willow baskets and espalier trees are grown along the walls. Admire this medieval-looking garden from one of the nearby benches.'

Flemish primitives in the spotlight

Till-Holger Borchert sees respect as the key to success

Groeningemuseum

He was born in Hamburg, he lives in Brussels and he thoroughly enjoys his work in Bruges as he finds himself surrounded by six centuries of fine arts, and especially the magnificent masterpieces of the Flemish primitives. In 2002, Till-Holger Borchert was one of the curators of Bruges, Cultural Capital of Europe. Today he is director-general of Musea Brugge chief curator of the Groeninge Museum and the Arentshuis. This year, together with Michel Dewilde, he is curator of the 2018 Triennial.

'Bruges is an exceptionally beautiful city,' says Till-Holger Borchert. 'What's more, it is also a wonderfully liveable place, partly because of the clever and careful way in which the city has been able to mix her medieval character with a modern ambiance. As early as the 13th century, the concentration of wealthy citizens enabled Bruges to become the commercial heart of Northwestern Europe. In the 15th century, the Burgundian authorities took successful structural measures, which resulted in an increase of the population and had a positive effect on the city's further development. Just as importantly, Bruges was spared the many ravages of the so-called Iconoclastic Fury, which caused so much damage in other cities. That spirit of respect and tolerance still pervades the city today. I must say it is a great joy to be here. The countless locals and visitors will surely fully agree with me.'

Madonnas from around the Corner

'Nearly every day I go and greet two masterpieces: Hans Memling's *Madonna and Maarten van Nieuwenhove* at the Saint John's Hospital and Jan van Eyck's *Madonna with Canon Joris van der Paele* at the Groeninge Museum. I am not saying that I discover something new every time I look at them, but my curiosity and my pleasure remain as great as ever. And I still try and find out new things about them. They just continue to fascinate me! I sometimes wonder why peo-

MUSEUM SHOP

'Whoever enters the museum shop of the Groeninge Museum will leave with some wonderful memories, that I can assure you. Perhaps you will take home your favourite art treasures in the shape of a handsomely illustrated book or a reproduction on a poster maybe, or depicted on a few picture postcards. And why don't you surprise yourself with an original souvenir? I have caught not only some of my delighted fellow curators buying just such a present for themselves, but my wife as well!'

ple from all corners of the world have always found the Flemish primitives so absorbing. The answer perhaps lies in the fact that for the very first time in art history we are confronted with recognisable people and familiar objects that correspond to today's reality. Even a Madonna seems to look like the woman from around the corner. The Flemish primitives laid the foundation of an artistic concept that in its realism is perfectly recognisable and therefore understandable to a modern-day observer. The Flemish primitives discovered the individual. Quite a feat. Those Flemish painters were also dab hands at solving problems. They explored space in an incredibly skilful and sophisticated way, for example by placing a mirror somewhere in the room. In Memling's diptych,

'Nearly every day I go and greet two masterpieces.'

a round mirror on the left-hand side behind the Madonna reflects the interior she is sitting in. In it, her own portrait is painted just a whisker away from the silhouette of the patrician Maarten van Nieuwenhove, Memling's patron. Truly magnificent. Are these works of art still capable of moving me? Absolutely. For pure emotion, a painter like Rogier van der Weyden touches me more deeply than Jan van Eyck. The works of van Eyck or Memling impress me more with their intellectual and conceptual qualities. Van der Weyden and van Eyck: it is worth visiting the treasure houses of Bruges, even if only for the pleasure of enjoying these two opposite ends of the artistic spectrum.'

INTERESTING TOMBS

The central feature in the Jerusalem Chapel – located in the Saint-Anne district – is the ceremonial tomb of Anselm Adornes (1424-1483) and his wife, Margareta Vander Banck (d. 1462). Anselm – scion of a wealthy merchant family, confidant of the dukes of Burgundy and a counsellor of the King of Scotland – had this chapel built in the likeness of the Church of the Holy Sepulchre in Jerusalem, with the intention that he should be buried here with his spouse. However, Anselm was killed and buried in Scotland.

Only his heart was later added to the tomb in Bruges. The decorative tombstone depicts Anselm and Margareta 'en gisant': lying stretched out with their heads on a cushion and their hands folded in prayer. Anselm is dressed as a knight, with a lion at this feet, symbolizing courage and strength. Margareta is dressed as a noblewoman; at her feet rests a dog, symbolizing faithfulness.

Till-Holger Borchert
Best addresses

FAVOURITE SPOT

» The churches of Bruges

'The great churches of Bruges possess wonderful art collections, containing pieces that wouldn't disgrace any top museum. Look up at the sheer breath-taking height of the Church of Our Lady, whose 115.5-metre high tower is the second tallest brick-built tower in the world. When in Saint Saviour's, do go and marvel at the frescoes in the baptistery. And Saint-James's Church is worth its while for the impressive **mausoleum of the de Gros family**, because this sculptural masterpiece reveals par excellence the self-confidence and power of the Burgundian elite.'

RESTAURANTS

» Den Gouden Harynck, Groeninge 25, tel. +32 (0)50 33 76 37, www.goudenharynck.be

'Den Gouden Harynck is a household name in Bruges, known and loved by foodies of all kinds. It is also one of the most pleasant star-rated restaurants in the city – as anyone who has ever been there will tell you.'

» Rock-Fort, Langestraat 15, tel. +32 (0)50 33 41 13, www.rock-fort.be

'Rock-Fort serves original, contemporary dishes with a modern twist. Their cooking is so good that the place is packed all week long. Local people love it, and I also like to pop in from time to time. But be careful: it is closed during the weekends.'

» **Den Amand**, Sint-Amandsstraat 4, tel. +32 (0)50 34 01 22,
www.denamand.be

'In Den Amand, I once saw a German restaurant critic copy out the entire menu card. You can't get higher praise than that! A small and elegant bistro, where you will find both tourists and local people enjoying the excellent food.'

» **'t Schrijverke**, Gruuthusestraat 4, tel. +32 (0)50 33 29 08, www.tschrijverke.be

'This homely restaurant is named after a poem by Guido Gezelle, which hangs in a place of honour next to the door. But 't Schrijverke is above all rightly famed for its delicious regional dishes and its *Karmeliet* beer on tap.'

» **Tanuki**, Oude Gentweg 1, tel. +32 (0)50 34 75 12, www.tanuki.be

'A true temple of food where you immediately drop your voice to the level of a whisper, so that you don't disturb the silent enjoyment of the other diners. In the open kitchen the chef does magical things with sushi and sashimi, and prepares his seven course menus with true oriental serenity.'

CAFÉS

» **Café 't Klein Venetië**, Braamberg-straat 1, tel. +32 (0)50 33 10 37,
www.kleinvenetie.be

'Every Bruges local knows that if you want to enjoy the sun, the terrace of Café 't Klein Venetië is the best place to go. I like to sit here on the front row, enjoying the busy crowds on the Huidenvettersplein and the magnificent view over the Rozenhoedkaai, the most photographed spot in Bruges. In short, when you are on this super-popular terrace, you never know where to look first.'

» **Delaney's Irish Pub & Restaurant**, Burg 8, tel. +32 (0)50 34 91 45,
www.delaneys.be

'It's always party time in this Irish pub, with its distinctive international atmosphere. Delaney's is the kind of place where you can rub shoulders with the whole world at the bar.'

» **The Druid's Cellar**, Sint-Amandsstraat 11, tel. +32 (0)50 61 41 44,
www.thedruidscellar.eu

'I like to drop in at The Druid's Cellar every now and again, even if only to watch Drew, my favourite barkeeper, in action. Or simply to relax and enjoy a glass from their wide range of Scottish and Irish whiskies. They always taste just that little bit better in The Druid's.'

» **Café Marcel**, Niklaas Desparsstraat 7-9, tel. +32 (0)50 33 55 02,
www.hotelmarcel.be

'Café Marcel is Bruges' refined version of a contemporary vintage café, but in a tight, new design setting. Think of dark wooden floorboards, simple lamps, leather benches and original wood panelling. You can pop in here for a tasty breakfast or an aperitif with tapas.'

» **Hollandse Vismijn**, Vismarkt 4, tel. +32 (0)50 33 33 01

'Whenever I fancy one of the popular Belgian beers, you will probably find me in the Hollandse Vismijn. This cheap and cheerful 'people's pub' is on the Fish Market. It is the type of café where everybody knows everybody and where you always get a warm welcome. Cheers!'

SHOPPING LIST

» **D's Deldycke traiteurs**, Wollestraat 23, tel. +32 (0)50 33 43 35,
www.deldycke.be

'In the 15th century, the Spaniard Pedro Tafur was already praising Bruges for its wide available selection of exotic fruits and rare spices. The Deldycke caterer is proud to continue this centuries-old tradition. Here, all your culinary wishes will be fulfilled.'

» **Antiquariaat Van de Wiele**, Sint-Salvatorskerkhof 7, tel. +32 (0)50 33 63 17,
www.marcvandewiele.com

'For art and history, I was fortunate enough to discover Marc Van de Wiele Antiques. This is undoubtedly one of the best addresses in a city that is rich in antique shops. The place to find unique, illustrated books from days long gone by.'

» **Boekhandel De Reyghere**, Markt 12, tel. +32 (0)50 33 34 03, www.dereyghere.be

'For all my other reading material I rely on De Reyghere, located on the Market Square. Foreign visitors feel instantly at home in this book and newspaper store, primarily because of the large number of international titles it has on sale.'

» **Den Gouden Karpel**, Vismarkt 9-10-11, tel. +32 (0)50 33 33 89, www.dengoudenkarpel.be

'The fishing family Ameloot have been running Den Gouden Karpel with heart and soul for many years: not only an excellent catering service and fishmongers, but also a top-class fish bar, where you can enjoy the very best seafood (*fruits de mer*). For a fish-lover like myself, it is hard to walk past Den Gouden Karpel without stopping to buy something.'

» **Parallax**, Zuidzandstraat 17, tel. +32 (0)50 33 23 02, www.parallax.be

'I always buy my socks at Parallax, but they are also experts at stylishly camou-flaging my beer belly! Highly recommended for other fashion victims and the ves-timentally challenged! Boss, Scabal, Zilton, Falke: you can find them all here.'

SECRET TIP

» **Museumshop**, Hof Arents, Dijver 16, www.museabrugge.be

» **Jerusalem Chapel**, **Gezelle Museum**, **Lace Centre**, **Church of Our Lady of the Pottery** and **Museum of Folk Life**: *see pages 54, 62, 64, 66 and 73 for more information.*

'Whenever I want to take a breather, I saunter down Saint Anne's, Bruges' most striking working-class neighbour-hood. You can still sense the charm of an authentic community in the streets around the **Museum of Folk Life**. The area boasts many fascinating places, too. Off the cuff, if I may: Our Lady of the Pottery, the Lace Centre, the medieval Jerusalem Chapel and the Gezelle Museum.'

Cultural capital Bruges

Albert Edelman fills the Concert Hall

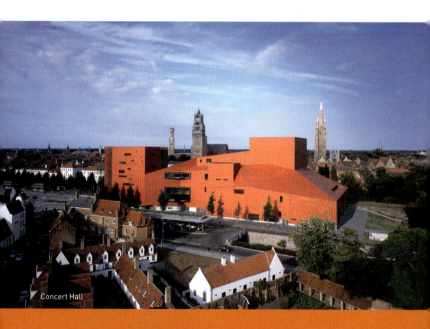

Concert Hall

Each year, the Bruges Concert Hall continues to attract an increasingly bigger and more diverse audience, and this is partly the merit of Albert Edelman. As artistic coordinator for Early Music, he manages to lure the very best ensembles to Bruges; a matter, he says, of pleasing both the local people and the tourists musically.

ID-CARD

Name: Albert Edelman
Nationality: Dutch
Date of birth: 3 October 1978
Has lived in Bruges since 2011. Albert is artistic coordinator for Early Music at the Concert Hall.

The Belgians and the Dutch may speak the same language, but that does not necessarily mean they always understand each other. Albert Edelman discovered this for himself in 2011, when he exchanged the Early Music Festival in Utrecht, the Netherlands, for a job as artistic coordinator for Early Music at the Bruges Concert Hall. 'During the first weeks, I really had difficulty understanding people. When my local baker spoke to me each morning, I just stood there with a smile. But that's all behind me now. Flemish people think a bit longer before saying something, and I like that. There is also more distance between people here than is customary in the Netherlands. The locals in Bruges need more time to get to know someone, which is not a bad thing, and I love that. Yes, I like it here a lot.' In the meantime, Albert now feels fully at home in Bruges and each morning, just like his fellow citizens, he cycles cheerfully to work. 'I live near the Sint-Anna canal, so my 'commuting' is extremely picturesque. A beautiful panoramic picture, with the Bruges Belfry as one of the highlights: 83 metres tall and comprising 47 bells, 27 tons of bronze and more than 500 years of carillon history.'

Different styles, no compromises

Add to this a varied, challenging job and his joy is complete! 'There are relatively few concert halls that pay as much attention to 'my' kind of music as the Bruges Concert Hall. Right from the very beginning, it was clear that early and contemporary music would both have a place here. This results in a very diverse programme; we bring a multiplicity of different styles, but we always try to tell a story with what we offer. In my opinion, music played on old instruments truly belongs in a historical city like Bruges: it is like an echo of what once has been. What's more, the musical opportunities offered by the Concert Hall itself are outstanding; its acoustics are absolutely top-draw. We can pres-

'You can also see that a long cultural tradition already exists in Bruges. This leads to an exciting interaction.'

ent all different kinds of genres, from chamber music to a capella, without having to compromise. Everything sounds good in the Concert Hall. Technically, the sound quality is always perfect, which is very unusual. In short, this is the place where you can enjoy music and dance in the best possible circumstances.' And Albert also does plenty of enjoying of his own: 'I know less about contemporary music and dance, which is why I am making grateful use of my stay in Bruges to discover the delights of these genres.'

'We have a very good and loyal public. People who are curious, who want to hear new things and follow our tips. We work with reasonable ticket prices so that we can reach a wider audience. In the foyer before a performance, you will see distinguished gentlemen in suits rubbing shoulders with young people in jeans. Everyone feels welcome here, whether they are local people or tourists. People genuinely come for the music – and not to be seen – which really pleases me.' 'You can also see that a long cultural tradition already exists in Bruges. This leads to an exciting interaction. We challenge the audience, and in return they let us know what they want to hear and see.' In order to keep

THE MUSICAL EVENT LIST OF ALBERT EDELMAN

1. 'The **Bruges MAfestival** is one of the world's most famous festivals for Early Music. For ten days, a surprising range of concerts is organised at different locations in the city and its immediate surroundings. In addition, there are also numerous readings, workshops and master classes.'
    (For more information about the MAfestival see page 81) www.mafestival.be

2. 'The **Bach Academie**, in collaboration with Philippe Herreweghe, has become a firm favourite with Bach lovers all over the world. About 30% of the visitors come from abroad. Each year, the festival weekend attracts leading international musicians and ensembles who specialize in the incomparable oeuvre of Johann Sebastian Bach.'
    (For more information about the Bach Academy see page 78)
    www.concertgebouw.be

3. 'Thee **concerts of Anima Eterna Brugge**. This fantastic orchestra explores the classic, Romantic and early modern repertoire. They perform on historical instruments and with great respect for the original intentions of the composer.'
    www.animaeterna.be

BRUGES AND THE CARILLON: A SHARED HISTORY

The very first bells were developed in China, around 2000 B.C. The art of bell-making was then brought to the Roman Empire via Egypt and Greece, and from there arrived in Northern Europe around 400 A.D. Bells were soon used as a means to call the faithful to prayer and to warn the population of approaching danger. Charlemagne made the use of bells in a belfry obligatory at the end of the 8th century. Towards the end of the 13th century, bells were attached to mechanical mechanisms for the first time. In the 16th century, rich cities like Bruges added grandeur to their belfries and church towers by adding more and more bells. And so the carillon - the oldest (and biggest) musical mass medium in history - was born! In the 17th century, the technique was refined and since the 18th century the carillon, which officially must have at least 23 bells, has functioned as an independent musical instrument. Since the beginning of the 20th century, the art of carillon playing has undergone international expansion. In November 2014, UNESCO recognized Belgian carillon culture as an intangible item of world cultural heritage. The Bruges Belfry boasts a **triumphal bell** from 1680, which is two metres in diameter and weighs 6 tons. The bells in the current carillon largely date from the 18th century and were recently renovated. For more than 500 years, bell music has rung out across the city. On Monday and Wednesday evenings in summer, the free concerts attract lots of people to the inner courtyard of the Belfry. The carillon also plays every Wednesday, Saturday and Sunday from 11.00 a.m. to 12.00 p.m.

that audience captivated, Albert regularly goes on reconnaissance trips. 'I have the opportunity to see and hear many new things, both here and abroad. This way, I keep up to date with everything happening in the music world. By meeting other musicians, it is possible to make plans together, which in turn often leads to unique custom written programmes that are mainly performed in Bruges. In addition, I am constantly searching for young, fresh talent. Many young people are active in music from the Middle Ages, the Renaissance and the Baroque period, so there are plenty of new initiatives. In my mind, there is no doubt: Early Music is alive and kicking, more so than ever before! And certainly in Bruges!'

(Learn more about the Concert Hall with the Concertgebouw Circuit, see page 53)

Albert Edelman
Best addresses

FAVOURITE SPOT

» **Sint-Janshospitaal (St. John's Hospital)**, Mariastraat 38, tel. +32 (0)50 44 87 43, www.museabrugge.be

'The **St. John's Hospital** does not display too many pieces, so that attention can be focused on the six Memlings in the collection. The impressive attic is ideal for performances and exhibitions.'
(See also pages 69-70)

RESTAURANTS

» **Bhavani**, Simon Stevinplein 5, tel. +32 (0)50 33 90 25, www.bhavani.be

'A little piece of Bombay in the Simon Stevin Square. Here you can enjoy the more refined Indian cooking, whether in summer on the terrace or in winter around the cosy open fire. And Ganesh saw that it was good.'

» **Bistro Bruut**, Meestraat 9, tel. +32 (0)50 69 55 09, www.bistrobruut.be
'In a short space of time, this place has become a reference for every Bruges foodie. In here, you can enjoy a delicious meal in a simple setting with a relaxed atmosphere. Top gastronomy without frills.'

» **Refter**, Molenmeers 2, tel. +32 (0)50 44 49 00, www.bistrorefter.com
'Whoever wants to eat gastronomically without paying astronomically is definitely at the right address. What's more, this affordable bistro owned by top chef Geert Van Hecke has a heavenly terrace.'

» **Bistro Christophe**, Garenmarkt 34, tel. +32 (0)50 34 48 92,
  www.christophe-brugge.be

'This evening and night bistro serves French classics and seasonal suggestions
until the early hours. Ideal for anyone who wants a nice dinner after a show.'

» **Osteria 45**, Sint-Jakobsstraat 45, tel. +32 (0)50 69 83 07, www.osteria45.be

'Osteria 45 not only serves richly topped pizzas and fresh-made pasta, but you
can also get delicious cocktails, which makes the wait for your meal even more
enjoyable. The service is not typically Bruges – but typically Italian with singing!'

CAFÉS

» **Concertgebouwcafé**, 't Zand 34,
  tel. +32 (0)50 47 69 99,
  www.concertgebouw.be/cafe

'Of course, it is impossible for me to ex-
clude the Concert Hall café from this little list. It's the perfect place to hang out
before and after shows. You can also
pop in during the day to order one of the
suggestions or just have a coffee.'

» **Groot Vlaenderen**, Vlamingstraat 94, tel. +32 (0)50 68 43 56,
  www.grootvlaenderen.be

'A cocktail bar with the air of a chic hotel lobby. A place that could just as easily
be found in Hong Kong or New York. On top of that, the cocktails are perfect and
the seats incredibly comfortable.'

» **Craenenburg**, Markt 16, tel. +32 (0)50 33 34 02, www.craenenburg.be

'The Craenenburg is rightly proud of its unique terrace. It is also the best place
to hear the Belfry, Bruges' greatest and most beautiful musical instrument, in
all its glory.'

» **De Republiek**, Sint-Jakobsstraat 36, tel. +32 (0)50 73 47 64,
  www.republiekbrugge.be

'The Republiek recently rose, phoenix-like, from its ashes and now boasts a
brand new interior. Fortunately, the huge walled inner courtyard remains un-
changed. A pleasant spot to sit and chat, or simply to enjoy the sun.'

» **Monsieur Ernest**, Wulfhagestraat 43, tel. +32 (0)50 96 09 66,
www.monsieurernest.com

'The privileged location of this outstanding hotel bar is enough to make everyone's mouth water. Nervous about going inside? There's no need to be: non-
hotel guests are always more than welcome. It is the best way to enjoy the
Bruges canals in style!'

SHOPPING LIST

» **Le Pain de Sébastien**, Smedenstraat 31, tel. +32 (0)50 34 47 44,
www.lepaindesebastien.be

'There is bread and bread. Only the
best ingredients are good enough for
Sébastien Cailliau, and you can taste
that in every bite. This explains why
you always have to queue here every
Saturday.'

» **Café Costume**, Ezelstraat 10, tel. +32 (0)50 66 11 98, www.cafecostume.com
'Trendy and timeless made-to-measure suits of the very highest quality and tai-
loring skill. That is the trademark of Café Costume. From the basic material to
the lining and the cufflinks: you choose it all. The result is a garment that is truly
unique. Sometimes rock 'n roll, sometimes classic - but always with an exclusive twist.'

» **Vero Caffè**, Sint-Jansplein 9, tel.+32 (0)50 70 96 09
'This is the best address for anyone who really likes coffee. Add a rich choice of
teas and fresh, home-baked cakes and pastries, and my happiness is complete.'

» **De Corte**, Sint-Amandsstraat 28, tel. +32 (0)50 33 46 07, www.decortebrugge.be
'From students to businessmen: everyone finds their way to De Corte. It is the
address in Bruges for original, affordable yet top-quality pens, leatherware and
accessories. If you ever want to buy that exclusive Montblanc or a moleskin
notebook, this is the place to come.'

» Rombaux, Mallebergplaats 13,
tel. +32 (0)50 33 25 75,
www.rombaux.be

'Music fans can indulge themselves here to their heart's content. Browse through scores, pick out CDs or admire the wonderful interior; all is possible in Rombaux.'

SECRET TIP

» Lissewege

'I live in the Saint-Anne district, a lovely place, but **Lissewege** is also highly recommended. Each time the MAfestival takes place, you can find me there. Thanks to the impressive acoustics in the church, it is a fantastic location for concerts. The beautiful old barn in Ter Doest is also well worth a visit.'

For more information about the places of interest in 'the white village' Lissewege, see pages 56-57 and 65.

Focus on the Great War

Sharon Evans, in search
of the First World War

Hill 62 [Westhoek]

Just a handful of kilometres from Bruges lies the Westhoek region. This green and pleasant land is now a haven of peace, but one hundred years ago, between 1914 and 1918, it was the setting for some of the most terrible fighting the world has ever seen. It was the Westhoek that first brought Sharon Evans to Belgium many years ago. Nowadays, this Bruges 'settler' leads visitors on tours of the old battlefields.

ID-CARD

Name: Sharon Evans
Nationality: Australian
Date of birth: 9 September 1965
Has lived in Bruges since 1991. Sharon runs Quasimodo and organises bus trips to among other the Westhoek, where she gives guided tours to many hundreds of tourists.

Sharon was born in Asia, as the daughter of a serving Australian soldier. Having moved from place to place in that part of the world several times, she eventually decided that the time had come to see what things were like on the other side of the planet! A year later, her wanderlust had still not been satisfied, and so she decided to 'hang around for a bit longer' in Europe. The choice was between Bruges and Vienna. 'I felt that Bruges was smaller, prettier, cleaner and friendlier – and so I chose Flanders.' Today, many years later, this citizen of the world still lives and works in Bruges. Her very first visit to Belgium – and the reason why she was so determined to come to our little country –

'In the Westhoek I had the feeling that I was following in my great-grandfather's footsteps. Here in Flanders, I discovered a piece of my own history.'

BRUGES, OCCUPIED CITY

Less well-known – because the history of the Great War mainly focuses on places at the front – is the fact that during the First World War, Bruges was the German headquarters for operations on the Atlantic coast. Shortly after the German Marine Infantry had installed their occupation regime in the city, the German High Command decided to convert the harbour at Zeebrugge into a base for their submarine fleet. Bruges also served as a place of relaxation for the German Army and – for the officers, at least – as a place of culture. After serving at the front for a period of 3 to 6 months, German soldiers were allowed a stay of 2 to 4 weeks in Bruges, to rest and recuperate.

With the special app brugge1418, you can go in search of the remaining traces of the Great War in the city. You can find the app in the Playstore (Android) or the App Store (Apple).

RELIVE THE BATTLE FOR THE NORTH SEA
21/4/2018 to 31/8/2018

On 23 April 1918, St. George's Day, the British fought a large-scale naval action along the Belgian coast, hoping to destroy the heavily defended German submarine pens in the harbours at Zeebrugge and Ostend, from where U-boats were wreaking havoc among British ships in the North Sea. Relive the history of this day in the exhibition *14-18, the battle for the North Sea*, in the Provincial Court on the Market Square, which at the time was the nerve centre of the German operations. You can experience the stifling conditions on board a U-boat and the tension of the nocturnal British raids.
INFO > www.vliz.be/battle-for-the-north-sea

took Sharon to the Westhoek. This was the place where her great-grandfather, together with his many comrades, had fought side by side during the Great War. 'I am the daughter of a soldier, so I already knew quite a lot about the First World War. And I have always been interested in history; I guess it's just built into my genes! Besides, the Great War was very important for the Australian people. It's true that we lost many of our finest sons, but out of that suffering we discovered our identity as a nation.'

The fascinating Westhoek

On her very first day in Belgium, Sharon immediately set off for the Westhoek. 'It's a wonderful place, with an undulating and easy-going landscape.' It was also an emotional place for Sharon. 'I had the feeling that I was follow-

THE RAID ON ZEEBRUGGE

During the First World War, Zeebrugge – the outport of Bruges – was transformed into a highly sophisticated submarine base, with the intention of cutting off the overseas supply lines to England. As a result, the British decided to attack the harbour. On 23 April 1918, Saint George's Day, a flotilla under Vice-Admiral Keyes made an attempt to block the entrance to the harbour, so that the German U-boats could cause no further damage. This famous raid, one of the most high-risk operations during the entire war, is still commemorated each year.

ing in my great-grandfather's footsteps. Walking where he had walked, remembering how he had struggled and fought here all those years ago... It was a really moving and deeply personal experience. Here in Flanders, I discovered a piece of my own history. People who have never been here before find it hard to imagine that this delightful countryside was once a terrible battlefield, full of misery and death. In Tyne Cot Cemetery, the largest British military cemetery on the European mainland, there is a huge memorial wall engraved with the names of 35,000 soldiers who went 'missing', whose bodies were never found. 35,000! Something like that cannot fail to affect you. In the meantime, I have been back to the Westhoek thousands of times, but I will never forget that very first time. And no matter how often I come, it never ceases to make an impression. It's that kind of place; it gets under your skin...'

In 1991, Sharon founded the forerunner of Quasimodo. Originally, she offered her tourist customers both cycling and bus tours, but she eventually decided to concentrate on the latter. Today she runs Quasimodo with her husband, Philippe. The couple have two tours: *WWI Flanders Fields Tour* and *Triple Treat: the best of Belgium in one day.*
(For more information see www. quasimodo.be; for more information on the Westhoek, see pages 146-147)

Sharon Evans
Best addresses

FAVOURITE SPOT

» The canals around Bruges

'As soon as you leave the city, you find yourself in another world: a green paradise. Whoever follows the Bruges-Ghent Canal or the **Damse Vaart** (Damme Canal), exploring the region by bike, is treated to one picture-postcard scene after another. Not to be missed!'

RESTAURANTS

» **Tête Pressée**, Koningin Astridlaan 100, tel. +32 (0)470 21 26 27, www.tetepressee.be

'You can find this foodie paradise just outside the city centre, but Tête Pressée is well worth the small detour. You will have a fantastic meal, you can watch the chef in action, and afterwards buy your own supply of delicious

things from the adjacent food store. A varied address that it is a delight to visit.'

» **Narai Thai**, Smedenstraat 43, tel. +32 (0)50 68 02 56, www.naraithai.be

'The Narai Thai is another culinary hot-spot: both literally and figuratively! Here you can enjoy dishes ranging from the mildly spicy to punishingly peppery, and all set in a trendy lounge atmosphere. It's almost like being transported to the other side of the world, even if only for an hour or so.'

» **Taj Mahal**, Philipstockstraat 6, tel. +32 (0)489 11 19 98,
www.tajmahalrestaurant.be

'I was born in Asia, so of course I like piquant Asian food. I like to order my Indian curries from the Taj Mahal. Hot and spicy!'

» **De Vlaamsche Pot**, Helmstraat 3-5, tel. +32 (0)50 34 00 86,
www.devlaamschepot.be

'Eccentric, yet at the same time very traditionally Flemish. This sounds like a contradiction, but the Vlaamsche Pot somehow manages to blend these two extremes together. In this somewhat unusual setting you can enjoy *waterzooi*, meat stew (*karbonaden*) and mussels with chips.'

» **In 't Nieuw Museum**, Hooistraat 42, tel. +32 (0)50 33 12 80,
www.nieuw-museum.com

'Carnivores will just love In 't Nieuw Museum, where delicious hunks of meat are cooked over a charcoal grill. From spare ribs to best end of neck to prime steak. And all in a delightfully relaxed atmosphere. Perfect for families.'

CAFÉS

» **Lokkedize**, Korte Vulderssstraat 33,
tel. +32 (0)50 33 44 50,
www.bistrolokkedize.be

'One of my very favourite places. A pleasant bar where you can always enjoy some rhythm & blues, a bit of rock 'n roll or a classic chanson. There are regular live performances and the kitchen stays open really late.'

» **Gran Kaffee De Passage**, Dweerstraat 26, tel. +32 (0)50 34 02 32,
www.passagebruges.com

'Gran Kaffee De Passage is in a traffic-free street, right in the middle of town. This luxurious café bathes in a *fin de siècle* atmosphere and offers good local cooking and an impressive range of Belgian beers. This is a great address, both for a quick snack and a full meal.'

» 't Stokershuis, Langestraat 7, tel. +32 (0)50 33 55 88, www.stokershuis.com
'Small is beautiful: that could easily be the motto of 't Stokershuis. A traditional city bar in mini-format, with bags of atmosphere. A place you'll find really hard to leave!'

» Bistro Zwart Huis, Kuipersstraat 23, tel. +32 (0)50 69 11 40,
www.bistrozwarthuis.be
'This protected monument was built in 1642, and the facade and the medieval bar-room are truly impressive. You can enjoy a bite to eat, a glass of something pleasant and occasional live music.'

» Blend, Kuipersstraat 6-8, tel. +32 (0)497 17 20 85
'I love good wine and like to try new vintages, especially in a super-cool interior. So Blend is my kind of place. A warm and fun wine bar and wine shop where you find lots of top-quality wines, either to drink on site by the glass or take home by the case!'

SHOPPING LIST

» De Kaasbolle, Smedenstraat 11,
tel. +32 (0)50 33 71 54,
www.dekaasbolle.be

'Whoever likes a delicious piece of beautifully matured cheese should definitely make their way to De Kaasbolle. From creamy Lucullus, the house cheese, through Tartarin Cognac (a fresh cow's milk cheese with Turkish raisins, marinated in French brandy) to the authentic Greek feta marinade: every one is a real treat for your taste buds.'

» ShoeRecrafting, Langestraat 13, tel. +32 (0)50 33 81 01,
www.shoerecrafting.be
'Luc Decuyper learnt the cobbler's art at Delvaux and other famous names in the leather trade, and is the man I can always rely on when my shoes start showing signs of wear. This excellent craftsman obviously loves his work – and it really shows in the end result.'

» Jofré, Vlamingstraat 7, tel. +32 (0)50 33 39 60, www.jofre.eu
'Admittedly, this ladies clothing boutique is not the cheapest in town, but it has an excellent selection of timeless designs that are well worth the investment. The kind of shop that a woman could spend quite some time in!'

» Quicke, Zuidzandstraat 21-23, tel. +32 (0)50 33 23 00, www.quicke.be
'Quicke is a shop like no other, which has been a reference for shoes far beyond Bruges since the magical year 1900. Here you can find all the latest 'must-haves' from Tod's, Marc Jacobs, Barbara Bui, Hogan, Salvatore Ferragamo, Paraboot, Ralph Lauren... When you leave this shop, you really do step out in style!'

» Chocolatier Dumon, Eiermarkt 6, Walstraat 6 en Simon Stevinplein 11, tel. +32 (0)50 22 16 22, www.chocolatierdumon.be
'I have been a big fan of Dumon's traditionally-made, top-quality chocolate for years. The Bruges story of confectioner Stephan Dumon began in 1996 on the Eiermarkt. In the meantime, he has also opened a sales point in the Walstraat and an impressive shop on the Simon Stevinplein. But I remain faithful to his small and welcoming shop on the Eiermarkt, where the old saying "good things come in small packages" really applies!'

SECRET TIP

» City Theatre, Vlamingstraat 29, tel. +32 (0)50 44 30 60, www.ccbrugge.be
'For me, taking in a concert at the City Theatre (Stadschouwburg) is a real treat. Bruges **Royal City Theatre**, in the very heart of the old city, dates from 1869 and is an architectural masterpiece. Every time I visit, I never fail to enjoy the waves of red and gold in the palatial auditorium and the opulent splendour of the majestic foyer. Little wonder that the Bruges theatre is regarded as one of the best preserved city theatres in all Europe.'

Lissewege

Discoveries outside of **Bruges**

The other Flemish historical cities

Antwerp (Antwerpen)   82 km

Antwerp has a lot to offer: a beautiful cathedral and numerous imposing churches, a magnificent Central Station, the ground-breaking Museum on the River (MAS), the tranquil Rubens House, a delightful sculpture garden (Middelheim), a zoo with a history and so much more. Antwerp is also Belgium's fashion capital, home to many internationally renowned designers. That is why in the Scheldt city you will find dozens of exclusive boutiques, rubbing shoulders with fun bric-a-brac shops where you can browse for hours! Not surprisingly, the local 'Antwerpenaars' – who are fairly loud by nature – are extremely proud of their city.

INFO > www.visitantwerpen.be; there is a direct train connection between Bruges and Antwerp (journey time: ca. 1.30 hours; www.belgianrail.be).

Brussels (Brussel)   88 km

The whole world comes together in Brussels, with a different continent around every corner, from the exotic Matonge quarter to the stately elegance of the European institutions. The capital of Belgium has a vibrancy like no other and the formality of its 'hard' metropolitan structure is softened by the authentic, working-class ambiance of its more popular districts. In the shadow of the majestic Market Square, *Manneken-Pis* is permanently peeing. This diverse city reconciles the chic sophistication of the Zavel with the folksy informality of the Vossenplein. Royalty watchers rush eagerly to the Paleizenplein, art lovers can do their thing at one of the more than hundred museums and galleries, such as the Magritte Museum, the BOZAR (Museum of Fine Arts) or the Horta Museum, foodies hurry to the numerous food temples, and vin-

tage-lovers climb to the top of the Atomium. And in the city where both Tintin and the Smurfs were born, comic lovers will find more than 50 comic-strip walls and a renowned Comics Museum.

INFO > www.visit.brussels; there is a direct train connection between Bruges and Bruxelles-Central (Brussels-Central, journey time: ca. 1.00-1.15 hours; www.belgianrail.be).

Damme 6 km

Until the silting up of the tidal inlet Zwin, Damme was the transhipment port of Bruges. To reach the literary home of Tijl Uilenspiegel (Owlglass), you drive straight along the banks of the Damse Vaart (Damme Canal), one of the most beautiful pieces of nature in all Belgium. The canal is lined with magnificent poplars, some of which are over 100 years old. Their wind twisted trunks add to the charm of the setting. You can also experience their beauty from the water. The nostalgic paddle steamer *Lamme Goedzak* travels to and fro between the small medieval town and Bruges' Noorweegse Kaai (Norwegian Quay). And every second Sunday of the

month, Damme is transformed into one big book centre!

INFO > www.visitdamme.be; scheduled bus no. 43 (not on Saturdays, Sundays and public holidays, see www.delijn.be for the time schedule), bus stop: Damme Plaats; or by the paddle steamer Lamme Goedzak, www.bootdamme-brugge.be *(for more information see page 51)*. You can also easily cycle to Damme *(for bicycle rental points see pages 150-151)* or hire a scooter to ride there *(see page 158 for scooter rental points)*.

Ghent (Gent) 39 km

The people of Ghent have always been a bit rebellious. It's in their genes. They rose in revolt against Emperor Charles. As punishment, he made them walk through the streets with nooses around their necks. Ever since they have been known as 'noose wearers', a name they wear with pride. In Ghent you can find the medieval alongside the trendy. The centuries old Belfry stands majestically alongside the new City Hall. The picturesque Patershol district, with its narrow streets and fun restaurants, stands in the shadow of the imposing Gravensteen Castle. The city is creating an international gastronomic furore with its young star-rated chefs and as the veggie capital of Europe. Art-lovers will find their way to the world-famous *The Adoration of the Mystic Lamb* by the van Eyck brothers in St. Bavo's Cathedral or one of the many museums. The S.M.A.K. (contemporary art), the Design Museum, the MSK (fine arts) and the STAM (city museum) will

surprise you each season with top-class exhibitions. The festivals, cultural events and vibrant night life guarantee non-stop fun and ambiance in the student city. And when the sun goes down, the Light Plan comes into its own. Buildings, squares and streets are bathed in atmospheric light. The ideal moment to visit local people's favourite place: the Graslei and the Korenlei alongside the quite waters of the River Schelde.

INFO > www.visitgent.be; there is a direct train connection between Bruges and Ghent (Sint-Pieters) (journey time: ca. 30 min.; www.belgianrail.be).

Louvain (Leuven) 110 km

Louvain is without a doubt the number one student city in Belgium. Dozens of historic university buildings are spread all over the old city centre. Leuven can proudly boast the largest and oldest university in Belgium, founded as long ago as 1425. Notwithstanding its long history, Leuven is always open to innovation, as can be seen in several remarkable architectural projects, such as the station, the Stuk Art Centre, Het Depot, De Hoorn (The Horn) in the trendy Vaartkom district and the M-Museum Leuven. And

then there is Louvain, city of beer. With two breweries – the giant Stella Artois plant and the smaller, more local Domus brewery – located in the city centre and with several other traditional brewers nearby, there is no excuse not to relax for a few moments with a foaming pint. And what better place than on the Oude Markt (Old Market), possibly the world's longest bar...

INFO > www.visitleuven.be; there is a direct train connection between Bruges and Leuven (journey time: ca. 1.30 hours; www.belgianrail.be).

Malines (Mechelen) 90 km

Although the smallest of the Flemish art cities, Mechelen is well worth a visit. Exactly halfway between Antwerp and Brussels, Mechelen is more compact than its larger neighbours, but is equally well endowed with historical monuments and listed buildings, which allow you to relive the glory years of the Burgundian empire. The most well-known landmark is the proud St. Rombout's Cathedral. Its 97-metre high tower contains two sets of bells, which are regularly played by pupils of the Royal carillon school – the oldest and largest in the

world. In addition, the River Dijle meanders through the city, enclosed by the Zoutwerf (Salt Quay) with its 16th century wooden frontages and the Haverwerf (Oat Quay) with its pastel-coloured decorative facades. The imposing Lamot brewery complex nowadays serves as a congress and heritage centre and is beautifully renovated in a daring and contemporary architectural style. Other 'musts' are the former palace of Margaret of Austria, from where the Low Countries were once ruled, and the Hof van Busleyden, a 16th century mansion where you can visit the new city museum from March 2018 onwards.

INFO > www.visitmechelen.be; there is a train connection between Bruges and Malines, with a single change of trains in Gent-Sint-Pieters or Bruxelles-Midi (Brussels-South) (journey time: ca. 1.30-1.45 hours; www.belgianrail.be).

Ypres (Ieper) 46 km

Thanks to its flourishing cloth industry, Ypres, along with Bruges and Ghent, was one of the most powerful cities in Flanders in the 13th century. Its strategically important position in the Westhoek meant that the city was besieged on several occasions, resulting in the construction of strong defensive ramparts, which were further extended in the 17th century. Ypres also paid a heavy price during the First World War, when it was the scene of fierce fighting that left the city in ruins. It was rebuilt after the Armistice, and the most important buildings are exact copies of the originals. The In Flanders Fields Museum lets the witnesses of war tell their own personal stories. These little histories reveal the huge emotions that are so sadly typical of all conflicts. This allows visitors to experience the horror of the trenches and the bombardment of the city. Various (day) trips are organized from Bruges to Ypres and other sites of interest in the Westhoek *(see pages 146-147)*.

INFO > www.toerisme-ieper.be; there is a train connection between Bruges and Ypres, with a single change of trains in Courtrai (journey time: ca. 1.30 hours; www. belgianrail.be); from Ypres station, it is approximately a 10-minute walk to the main Market Square.

Bruges' wood- and wetlands

The Bruges' wood- and wetlands form a green belt around the city. Here time passes more slowly and living the good life is all that counts. There are several star-rated chefs in the area, as well as numerous passionate regional producers. Add to this the picturesque canals that criss-cross the region, the flat polders that are a paradise for cyclists and the many historical buildings surrounded by lush greenery, and you can soon see why the Ommeland is a place that will live long in your memory. The world heritage city of Bruges is the beating heart of the region; the nostalgic towns and villages that surround it are its soul. Burgundian strolls through romantic castles, soaking up the history in Damme, Lissewege or one of the other timeless villages: anything goes, but there are no 'musts'. Everything is chill. Perhaps it's time to recharge your batteries and enjoy the delights of the Bruges Ommeland to the full!

INFO > www.brugseommeland.be

Not to be missed

The Uilenspiegel Museum (Damme, 6 km, www.visitdamme.be), the home of Tijl Uilenspiegel and his Nele; the Lamme Goedzak (Damme, 6 km, www.bootdamme-brugge.be; *see also*

Damme

GUIDED TOURS THROUGH BRUGES' WOOD- AND WETLANDS

Nothing is quite so much fun as discovering the area of the wood- and wetlands around Bruges - known locally as the Ommeland - with a guided tour. Bike-lovers can choose between the Green Bike Tour (arlando@telenet.be), Pink Bear Bike Tours (www.pinkbear.freeservers.com), Steershop gravel biketours (www.steershop.be) or QuasiMundo Biketours Brugge (www.quasimundo.eu). Alternatively, you can opt for a minibus tour with Quasimodo Tours (www.quasimodo.be) or a scooter ride with Vespa Tours (www.vespatours-brugge.be).

Damse Vaart

TIP

The ideal way to discover the surroundings of Bruges is by bike. Make your own route using the cycle network maps or follow the signposted Groene Gordel (Green Belt) cycle route. You can buy cycle routes in the **i** tourist information offices or on shop.westtoer.be
(See pages 150-151 for bicycle rental points)

page 51), a nostalgic paddle steamer that sails between Bruges and Damme; Loppem Castle (Loppem, 6 km, www.kasteelvanloppem.be), where King Albert I resided during the liberation of Belgium at the end of the First World War; the Permeke Museum (Jabbeke, 10 km, www.muzee.be), where you can stroll around the home, garden and workshops of the renowned painter Constant Permeke; the Roman Archaeological Museum (Romeins Archeologisch Museum - RAM) (Oudenburg, 16 km, www.ram-oudenburg.be), where you can marvel at the archaeological finds from Oudenburg's glorious past;

Wijnendale castle (Torhout, 18 km, www.toerismetorhout.be), home to more than a thousand years of history and a place of sad memories for King Leopold III; the Torhout Pottery Museum (Torhout, 18 km, www.toerismetorhout.be), which focuses on the rich tradition of the world-famous Torhout earthenware; and Ten Putte Abbey and farm (Gistel, 30 km, www.gistel.be), home to a group of nuns from the congregation of Our Mother of Peace. There is also the well-kept Godelieve Museum, where you can learn more about the remarkable life of Gistel's very own saint.

Loppem Castle

Wijnendale Castle

Coast

The Coast never loses its appeal. From De Panne to Knokke-Heist, each seaside resort has its own unique atmosphere. Old-world or contemporary, picturesque or chic, intimate or urbane, the seaside towns are all purveyors of the good life. Nature galore, an abundance of culture, wonderful sandy beaches, inviting shopping streets, traffic-free promenades that are ideal for a bracing seaside stroll: this is the Coast in a nutshell! And the regular tram service (www.dekusttram.be) allows you to travel from one resort to another in no time at all. Taste that salty sea air, enjoy the mild climate and treat yourself to a delicious meal with the very best the North Sea has to offer.

INFO > www.dekust.be

Not to be missed

During the Heritage Walk in Zeebrugge (shop.westoer.be) you will learn about the sea port of Bruges. The route (follow the studs in the ground) highlights the role of Zeebrugge in the Flemish fishing industry and in the First World War. Or perhaps you prefer to see the harbour from the water? The harbour tour on the passenger boat 'Zephira (Zeebrugge, 14 km, www.franlis.be, *see also page 51*) takes you through one of the world's biggest

Zeebrugge

BEAUFORT
30/3/2018 – 30/9/2018

Beaufort is synonymous with contemporary art on the Belgian coast. The sixth edition will again create surprising encounters with modern art in a series of unique settings along the sea. Discover the intriguing works of internationally respected artists in the parks, squares, promenades and beaches of some of Belgium's best-loved coastal towns.

INFO > www.beaufort18.be and www.dekust.be

locks. And why not visit Seafront (Zeebrugge, 14 km, www.seafront.be, *see also page 68*), a maritime theme park where you can unlock the secrets of the sea? In the Belle Epoque Centre in Blankenberge (Blankenberge, 14 km, www.belle.epoque.blankenberge.be) you can explore this exciting transition period between the 19th and 20th centuries, a carefree world of grandeur and luxury along the Belgian coast. In Ostend, Mu.ZEE is a 'must-see' (Ostend, 22 km, www.muzee.be), with its unique collection of modern and contemporary Belgian art and a brand-new wing devoted to the work of grandmasters James Ensor and Léon Spilliaert. From the end of 2018, you can also visit the renovated Ensor House (Ostend, 22 km, www.muzee.be), discovering the fascinating world of Ostend's most famous artist in a new experience centre and in the newly opened rooms where the painter once lived and worked.

Zeebrugge

Zeebrugge, Heritage Walk

Westhoek

Endless panoramic views, gently rolling hills, flat polders and a breath-taking silence. The landscape where the terrible battles of the Great War were once fought are now a calm and peaceful natural paradise with limitless pleasure. This green region, sandwiched between the French border and the North Sea coast, is dotted with numerous picturesque villages, where you can not only discover the sad history and the silent witnesses of the First World War, but also enjoy a bite to eat and a refreshing drink at one of the many charming restaurants and taverns, often located in the most idyllic settings. A joy for walkers and cyclists. Why not sample a Picon, the delicious borderland aperitif? One thing is certain; wherever you go and whatever you do, you will always be welcomed with the same West Flanders friendliness.
INFO > www.toerismewesthoek.be, www.flandersfields.be

Not to be missed

The In Flanders Fields Museum (Ypres, 46 km, www.inflandersfields.be), housed in the historic Cloth Hall in the centre of Ypres, tells in an impressively modern and interactive manner the tragic story of the First World War in the West Flanders front region. From June 2018 onwards, you can also visit the new Yper Museum (Ypres, 46 km, www.ypermuseum.be) in the same building, devoted to the past, present and future of this historic city which somehow al-

Ypres, Last Post

GUIDED EXCURSIONS TO THE WESTHOEK

Make a poignant but memorable (mini-)bus tour, leaving from Bruges, through the countless reminders of the First World War in the Westhoek, with Quasimodo Tours (www.quasimodo.be), the In Flanders Fields tour (www.brussels-city-tours.be) or Flanders Fields Battlefield Daytours (www.visitbruges.org).
(Also read the interview with Sharon Evans about the Westhoek on pages 128-131)

Zonnebeke, Memorial Museum Passchendaele

Lo-Reninge, Jules Destrooper Visitors' Centre

ways seems to land on its feet. Also in Ypres is the Last Post Ceremony (Ypres, 46 km, www.lastpost.be), a daily tribute to the dead of the Great War, which takes place at 8 o'clock sharp each evening at the Menin Gate, an imposing memorial that bears the names of 54,896 British soldiers whose bodies could not be identified. In the same way, Tyne Cot Cemetery (Passendale, 54 km, www.passchendaele.be, www.cwgc. org), the largest British military cemetery in Europe, makes tangible the immense human cost of the First World War. In the Memorial Museum Passchendaele 1917 (Zonnebeke, 66 km, www.passchendaele.be) you can learn more about what the soldiers experienced and walk through a reconstructed trench of the kind they would have known.

For families with children, Beauvoorde Castle (Wulveringem, 56 km, www. kasteelbeauvoorde.be) is well worth a visit. Here, you will be transported back to the romantic age of knights and their damsels, and can also enjoy one of the many family activities organized in the elegant castle park in the Anglo-French style. The Jules Destrooper Visitors' Centre (Lo-Reninge, 70 km, www.jules-destrooper.com) leads you through the rich history of this biscuit-making family and rewards you at the end of your visit with a sample tasting. Equally tasty is the Hop Museum in Poperinge (Poperinge, 83 km, www.hopmuseum. be), where you can learn everything you ever wanted to know about hops, which, you may be surprised to discover, are used for much more than just making beer!

Passendale, Tyne Cot Cemetery

Tourist office 't Zand (Concert Hall)

Bruges
practical

Practical information

Accessibility

If you see the wheelchair icon ♿ in this guide, it means that some provision has been made for disabled people. For more details about the different levels of accessibility at different places in Bruges, you can pick up a free brochure (in Dutch or English) from the ℹ️ info-offices.

Bicycle rental points

» 🚲 📶 **Bauhaus Bike Rental**
LOCATION > Langestraat 145
PRICE > 3 hours: €6; full day: €10
OPEN > Daily, 8.00 a.m.-8.00 p.m.
INFO > Tel. +32 (0)50 34 10 93,
www.bauhaus.be/services/bike-rental

» 🚲 **B-Bike Concertgebouw**
LOCATION > Concert Hall, 't Zand
PRICE > 1 hour: €4; 5 hours: €8; full day: €12. Tandem, 5 hours: €14; full day: €22. Electric bike, full day: €20
OPEN > 1/3 to 31/10: daily, 10.00 a.m.-7.00 p.m.; 1/11 to 28/2: open by appointment only
INFO > Tel. +32 (0)479 97 12 80,
www.bensbike.be

» 🚲 **Bruges Bike Rental**
LOCATION > Niklaas Desparsstraat 17
PRICE > 1 hour: €4; 2 hours: €7; 4 hours: €10; full day: €13, students (on display of a valid student card): €10. Electric bike, 1 hour: €10; 2 hours: €15; 4 hours: €22, full day: €30. Tandem, 1 hour: €10; 2 hours: €15; 4 hours: €20; full day: €25, students (on display of a valid student card): €22
OPEN > 1/2 to 31/12: daily, 10.00 a.m.-8.00 p.m.
ADDITIONAL CLOSING DATE > 25/12

INFO > Tel. +32 (0)50 61 61 08,
www.brugesbikerental.be

» 🚲 **De Ketting**
LOCATION > Gentpoortstraat 23
PRICE > Full day: €8. Electric bike, full day: €22
OPEN > 1/4 to 15/10: Monday to Saturday, 10.00 a.m.-6.00 p.m. and Sunday, 10.30 a.m.-6.00 p.m.; 16/10 to 31/3: Monday to Saturday, 10.00 a.m.-6.00 p.m.
INFO > Tel. +32 (0)50 34 41 96,
www.deketting.be

» 🚲 **Electric Scooters**
Rental of electric bikes.
LOCATION > Gentpoortstraat 55 and 62
PRICE > 2 hours: €10; 4 hours: €18; full day: €30
OPEN > 1/4 to 31/10: Monday, 1.00 p.m.-6.00 p.m., Tuesday to Saturday, 10.00 a.m.-6.00 p.m.
EXTRA > Rental of electric scooters *(see page 158)*
INFO > Tel. +32 (0)50 61 16 46 and +32 (0)475 94 20 02, www.electric-scooters.be

» 🚲 **Fietsen Popelier**
LOCATION > Mariastraat 26
PRICE > 1 hour: €5; 4 hours: €10; full day: €15. Electric bike or tandem, 1 hour: €10; 4 hours: €20; full day: €30
OPEN > 15/3 to 31/10: daily, 9.00 a.m.-7.00 p.m.; 1/11 to 14/3: daily, 10.00 a.m.-6.00 p.m.
ADDITIONAL CLOSING DATES >
1/1, 10/5 and 25/12; closed on Monday in January and December
INFO > Tel. +32 (0)50 34 32 62,
www.fietsenpopelier.be

» Fietspunt Station

LOCATION > Hendrik Brugmansstraat 3 (Stationsplein)
PRICE > 1 hour: €6; 4 hours: €10; full day: €15. Electric bike, 4 hours: €20; full day: €30
OPEN > Monday to Friday, 6.55 a.m-7.00 p.m.; 1/5 to 30/9: also during weekends and public holidays, 9.00 a.m.-5.00 p.m.
ADDITIONAL CLOSING DATES >
Closed for a number of days during the Christmas period; please contact the bicycle point in advance for details.
INFO > Tel. +32 (0)50 39 68 26, fietspunt.brugge@groepintro.be

» Koffieboontje
LOCATION > Hallestraat 4
PRICE > 1 hour: €5; 4 hours: €10; full day: €15, students (on display of a valid student card): €11.25. Tandem, 1 hour: €10; 4 hours: €20; full day: €30, students (on display of a valid student card): €22.50
OPEN > Daily, 9.00 a.m.-10.00 p.m.
INFO > Tel. +32 (0)50 33 80 27, www.bikerentalkoffieboontje.be

» La Bicicleta
LOCATION > Wijngaardstraat 13
PRICE > Full day: €15
OPEN > Daily, 11.00 a.m.-10.00 p.m., book in advance via the website.
INFO > Tel. +32 (0)478 33 49 69, www.labicicleta.be

» Snuffel Hostel
LOCATION > Ezelstraat 42
PRICE > Full day: €8
OPEN > Daily, 8.00 a.m.-8.00 p.m.
INFO > Tel. +32 (0)50 33 31 33, www.snuffel.be

» Steershop
LOCATION > Koolkerkse Steenweg 7a
PRICE > Full day: €10
OPEN > Tuesday to Saturday, 8.00 a.m.-

11.00 a.m. and 4.00 p.m.-8.00 p.m. (Saturday until 6.00 p.m.)
EXTRA > Guided tours *(see page 142)*
INFO > Tel. +32 (0)474 40 84 01, www.steershop.be

Most of the bicycle rental points ask for the payment of a guarantee.

🚲 Bike taxi
A bike taxi will bring you to your destination in an ecological way.
BIKE TAXI STANDS
» Markt (near the Historium)
» 't Zand (near the Concert Hall)
» Stationsplein (Kiss&Ride)
PRICE > Rates can be obtained (on-site) from the individual taxi companies.
INFO > Tel. +32 (0)472 67 35 25 or www.taxifietsbrugge.be, tel. +32 (0)478 40 95 57 or www.fietskoetsenbrugge.be and tel. +32 (0)478 51 41 15 or www.greenrides.eu

P 🚐 Campers
The Kanaaleiland ('Canal Island') at the Bargeweg offers an excellent camping site for at least 57 camping cars all year round. Once your camper is parked, you are just a five-minute walk from the city centre (via the Beguinage). It is not possible to make prior reservations.
PRICE > 1/4 to 30/9: €25/day; 1/10 to 31/3: €19/day. Free electricity; it is also possible to stock up on free clean water (€0.50) and dispose of dirty water.
OPEN > You can enter the site until 10.00 p.m. You can leave at any time.
INFO > www.interparking.com

Church services

01 **Basiliek van het Heilig Bloed (Basilica of the Holy Blood)**
Daily, except Mondays: 11.00 a.m.

02 Begijnhofkerk (Beguinage Church)
Monday to Saturday: 11.00 a.m.,
Sundays and public holidays: 9.30 a.m.

04 English Convent
Wednesdays and Fridays: 7.45 a.m.

12 English Church
('t Keerske / Saint Peter's Chapel)
English language Anglican service,
Sundays: 6.00 p.m. (in winter: 5.00 p.m.)

10 Kapucijnenkerk (Capuchins Church)
Monday to Friday: 8.00 a.m.
(Tuesdays: also 6.00 p.m.),
Saturdays: 6.00 p.m., Sundays: 10.00 a.m.

**11 Karmelietenkerk
(Carmelites Church)**
Monday to Friday: 12.00 p.m.,
Sundays: 10.00 a.m.

**15 Onze-Lieve-Vrouwekerk
(Church of Our Lady)**
Saturdays: 5.30 p.m., Sundays: 11.00 a.m.

**16 Onze-Lieve-Vrouw-ter-Potteriekerk
(Church of Our Lady of the Pottery)**
Sundays: 7.00 a.m. and 9.30 a.m.

**17 Onze-Lieve-Vrouw-van-Blindekens-
kapel (Chapel of Our Lady of the Blind)**
First Saturday of the month: 6.00 p.m.

**18 Orthodoxe Kerk
HH. Konstantijn & Helena (Orthodox
Church Saints Constantin & Helen)**
Saturdays: 6.00 p.m., Sundays: 9.00 a.m.

19 Sint-Annakerk (Saint Anne's Church)
Sundays: 10.00 a.m.

20 Sint-Gilliskerk (Saint Giles' Church)
Sundays: 7.00 p.m.

**22 Sint-Jakobskerk
(Saint James's Church)**
Wednesdays and Saturdays: 7.00 p.m.

**23 Sint-Salvatorskathedraal
(Saint Saviour's Cathedral)**
Monday to Friday: 6.00 p.m.
(Wednesdays: also 9.00 a.m.),
Saturdays: 4.00 p.m., Sundays: 10.30 a.m.

**12 Verenigde Protestantse Kerk
(United Protestant Church)**
('t Keerske / Saint Peter's Chapel)
Sundays: 10.00 a.m.

**25 Vrije Evangelische Kerk
(Free Evangelical Church)**
Sundays: 10.00 a.m.

Cinemas

» All films are shown in their original language. Subtitles in Dutch and/or French are available when necessary.

15 Cinema Lumière
Sint-Jakobsstraat 36, www.lumierecinema.be

16 Kinepolis Brugge
Koning Albert I-laan 200, Sint-Michiels,
www.kinepolis.com | scheduled bus no. 27,
bus stop: Kinepolis

Discount cards
and combi-tickets

You can get discounts for your visits to various museums, sites of interest and attractions in Bruges if you use a discount card or combi-ticket. *You can find more info on page 74.*

Emergencies

» **European emergency number: tel. 112**
This free general number is used in all the member states of the European Union to call

for assistance from the police, fire brigade or ambulance service: daily, 24 hours a day.

Formalities

» Identity

An identity card or valid passport is necessary. An ordinary identity card is sufficient for most citizens of the European Union. If you arrive in Belgium from outside the European Union, you must first pass through customs. There are no border controls once inside the European Union. Check at the Belgian embassy or at the consulate in your home country in advance to find out exactly what documents you need.

» Health

Citizens of the European Union have access to necessary medical care through their own national health insurance card/document. This care is given under the same conditions as for the local Belgian population. You can obtain this card from your own national health service. Please note, however, that every member of the family must have his/her own card/document.

Getting there

Up-to-date information about access can be found on www.visitbruges.be

▶ By car

From the UK you can travel to Bruges by ferry or by Eurotunnel:

» **Hull (UK) – Zeebrugge (B)** with P&O Ferries (crossing: 1 night). Take the N31 from Zeebrugge to Bruges. Estimated distance Zeebrugge – Bruges is 17 km or 11 miles (30 min driving).

» **Dover (UK) – Dunkerque (F)** with DFDS Seaways (crossing: 2h00). Take the motorway E40 to Bruges. Estimated distance Dunkerque – Bruges is 76 km or 47 miles (1h driving).

» **Dover (UK) – Calais (F)** with P&O Ferries or DFDS Seaways (crossing: 1h30). Esti-mated distance Calais – Bruges is 120 km or 75 miles (1h30 driving).

» **Folkestone (UK) – Calais (F)** via Eurotunnel (35 min). Estimated distance Calais – Bruges is 120 km or 75 miles (1h30 driving).

A 30 kph zone is in force throughout the entire city centre. This means that you are forbidden at all times to drive faster than 30 kilometres per hour. Parking is for an unlimited time and is most advantageous in one of the two city centre car parks. *(For more information, see 'Parking')*

▶ 🚌 By bus

Several international coach companies organize connections to Bruges from important international transport hubs and foreign cities. The bus stops for these services are on the Sint-Michiels' side (Spoorwegstraat) of the main railway station.

» To and from transport hubs

From Brussels South Charleroi Airport **flibco.com** runs several direct services each day. **Ouibus** organizes direct services from and to Lille-Europe HST station. The journey times are arranged to match the times of the Eurostar trains and the TGV. **Flixbus** operates a daily service to and from Prague and Cracow, with stops at Frankfurt Airport (terminal 2) and Cologne Airport. Flixbus also has regular services to and from Paris, with stops at Lille-Europe HST station, Charles de Gaulle Airport and Orly Airport.

» To and from foreign cities

Ouibus runs several direct services each day

to and from Lille. **Flixbus** organizes services to and from London, Dortmund, Essen, Düsseldorf, Eindhoven, Prague, Cracow and Paris, stopping at different French and German cities along the different routes.

Eurolines also has regular connections to and from Bruges with London and Amsterdam (via Ghent and Utrecht).

It is recommended to always book your seat in advance (for some companies it is obligatory). See www.flibco.com, www.ouibus.com, www.flixbus.com and www.eurolines.eu for up-to-date information about arrival/departure times, fare prices and reservations.

▶ By train
›› National
There are from one to four direct services each hour between Bruges and the important train junctions at Antwerp, Ghent, Hasselt, Leuven and Brussels. Please consult www.belgianrail.be.

›› International
The station at Brussel-Zuid (Brussels South) is the Belgian hub for international rail traffic. Numerous high-speed trains arrive in Brussel-Zuid daily, coming from Paris (Thalys/Izy and TGV), Lille (Eurostar, TGV and Thalys), London (Eurostar), Amsterdam (Thalys and, from spring 2018, Eurostar) and Cologne (Thalys and ICE). There are three trains an hour from Brussels-South Station, which stop at Bruges on their way to Ostend, Knokke or Blankenberge. The travelling time between Brussel-Zuid and Bruges is approximately 1 hour.

▶ By plane
›› Via Brussels Airport-Zaventem
It is easy to travel from Brussels Airport-Zaventem to Bruges by train. Every day there is a direct hourly service to Bruges. In addition, many other trains from Brussels Airport-Zaventem regularly stop at Brussels-North, Brussels-Central or Brussels-South railway stations. From these three stations there are daily three trains an hour stopping at Bruges on their way to Ostend, Knokke or Blankenberge. Consult www.belgianrail.be for information about arrival-departure times and fare prices. For those who prefer to take a taxi, you can find all the relevant information on page 159.

›› Via Brussels South Charleroi Airport
This popular regional airport receives multiple low-cost flights every day from various

▶ How to get to Bruges?

departure	via	km	miles	time boat	time train	time bus	make a reservation
Amsterdam	Brussels-South/-Midi	253	157	-	± 3:10	-	www.thalys.com, www.eurostar.com (from spring 2018)
Brussels Airport-Zaventem	-	110	68	-	± 1:30	-	www.belgianrail.be
Brussels South Charleroi Airport	-	148	92	-	-	2:10	www.flibco.com
Ostend-Bruges Airport	Oostende	24	15	-	see page 155		www.delijn.be, www.belgianrail.be
Dover	Dunkerque	-	-	2:00	-	-	www.dfdsseaways.com
Dover	Calais	-	-	1:30	-	-	www.poferries.com, www.dfdsseaways.com
Hull	Zeebrugge	-	-	1 night	-		www.poferries.com
Lille Flandres	Kortrijk	75	47	-	± 1:47	-	www.b-europe.com
London St Pancras	Brussels-South/-Midi	-	-	-	± 3:25	-	www.eurostar.com

cities and regions in Europe. The flibco.com bus company (www.flibco.com) provides several direct shuttle bus services to and from the station in Bruges on a daily basis. For those who prefer to take a taxi, you can find all the relevant information on page 159.

» Via Ostend-Bruges Airport

The railway station at Ostend is just a 15-minute bus ride away. From here, there are at least three trains to Bruges each hour between 6.00 a.m. and 10.00 p.m., with final destinations in Eupen, Welkenraedt, Brussels Airport-Zaventem, Antwerpen-Centraal or Kortrijk. The train journey to Bruges takes about 15 minutes. Consult www.belgianrail.be for information about arrival-departure times and fare prices. For those who prefer to take a taxi, you can find all the relevant information on page 159.

» In Bruges

From the station in Bruges, you can travel every five minutes to your overnight accommodation address by De Lijn bus *(see 'Public transport')* or by taxi *(see 'Taxis')*.

Good to know

Don't let pickpockets ruin your shopping trip. Always keep your **wallet/purse** in a closed inside pocket, and not in an open handbag or rucksack. A golden tip for ladies: always close your handbag and wear it with the fastener against your body. Bruges is a lively, fun-loving city with great nightlife. Please bear in mind that it is prohibited to sell, give or serve **spirits** (whisky, gin, rum, vodka, etc.) to people under the age of 18 years. For people under the age of 16, this prohibition applies for all drinks with an alcohol content exceeding 0.5%. When purchasing alcohol, proof of age may be requested. All drugs – including cannabis – are prohibited by law in Belgium. Visiting Bruges means endless hours of fun, but please allow the visitors who come after you to enjoy their stay in a **clean** and **tidy** city: so always put your rubbish in a rubbish bin.

Inhabitants

On 1 January 2017, there were 19,443 inhabitants registered as living in the inner city of Bruges. The total population of Greater Bruges on the same date was 118,103.

🔒 Lockers

» Station (railway station)

Stationsplein | City map: C13

» **Historium**

Markt 1

Market days

» Mondays

8.00 a.m.-1.30 p.m. | Onder de Toren – Lissewege | miscellaneous

» Wednesdays

8.00 a.m.-1.30 p.m. | Markt | food and flowers

» Fridays

8.00 a.m.-1.30 p.m. | Market Square – Zeebrugge | miscellaneous

» Saturdays

8.00 a.m.-1.30 p.m. | Beursplein (from July 2018: back on 't Zand) | miscellaneous

» Sundays

7.00 a.m.-2.00 p.m. | Veemarkt, Sint-Michiels | miscellaneous

» Wednesday to Saturday

8.00 a.m.-1.30 p.m. | Vismarkt | fish

» Daily

During the period 15/3 to 15/11: 9.30 a.m.-

5.00 p.m.; during the period 16/11 to 14/3: 10.00 a.m.-4.00 p.m. | Vismarkt | artisanal products

» **Saturdays, Sundays, public holidays and bridge days in the period 15/3 to 15/11 + also on Fridays in the period June to September**
10.00 a.m.-6.00 p.m. | Dijver | antique, bric-à-brac and crafts

Medical help

» **Doctors, pharmacists, dentists and nursing officers on duty**
tel. 1733. For non-urgent medical help during the evening, night and at weekends.
» **Hospitals**
A.Z. St.-Jan > tel. +32 (0)50 45 21 11
A.Z. St.-Lucas > tel. +32 (0)50 36 91 11
St.-Franciscus Xaveriuskliniek >
tel. +32 (0)50 47 04 70
» **Poisons Advice Centre**
tel. +32 (0)70 245 245

Money

Most of the banks in Bruges are open from 9.00 a.m. to 12.30 p.m. and from 2.00 p.m. to 4.30 p.m. Many branch offices are also open on Saturday morning, but on Sundays they are all closed. There are cash points 🏧 in several shopping streets, on 't Zand, Simon Stevinplein, Stationsplein and on Bargeplein. You can easily withdraw money from cash machines with Visa, Eurocard or MasterCard. You can exchange money in one of the currency exchange offices. In the event of the loss or theft of your bank or credit card, it is best to immediately block the card by calling Card Stop on tel. 070 344 344 (24 hours a day).
» **Exchange office Goffin Change nv**
INFO > Steenstraat 2, tel. +32 (0)50 34 04 71
» **Exchange office Pillen bvba**
INFO > Vlamingstraat 18, tel. +32 (0)50 44 20 50

» **Exchange office Pillen R.W.J. bvba**
INFO > Rozenhoedkaai 2, tel. +32 (0)50 34 59 55

Opening hours

Cafés and restaurants have no (fixed) closing hour. Sometimes they will remain open until the early hours of the morning and other days they will close earlier: it all depends on the number of customers.
(See 'Shopping in Bruges' for info about shop opening times, page 88)

Parking

Bruges is a compact city, made for people. The use of motorized transport in the historic city centre is discouraged. There are a number of outlying car parks within easy walking distance of the centre where you can park **free of charge**. A little further away are the park-and-ride cark parks, also free, from which you can reach the centre by bike or public transport. A blue zone has been created around the city centre. You can park free of charge for a limited period in this blue zone (max. 4 hours) between 9.00 a.m. and 6.00 p.m. Always remember to use your parking disc! Above ground parking in the city centre is also possible for a limited period (max. 4 hours) between 9.00 a.m. and 8.00 p.m., but is paid (1 hour: €1.80; 2 or 3 hours: €2.40; 4 hours: €9). Payment can be made via an sms/text message, using the 4411 app or by cash or bank card at one of the parking ticket machines. The correct number plate of your car must always be entered into the machine in advance. Parking in the city centre for an unlimited period is **cheapest** in the public cark parks in front of the railway station (City Map: D13) and under the 't Zand square. Both car parks are within easy walking distance of the market square, or else you can use one of the city buses operated by De Lijn *(for more info, see the section on 'Public transport')*. The bus transfer (max. 4 people per car) from the station car park to the city centre and back is included in the price of the parking ticket. If you are staying overnight in Bruges, ask your hotel or guesthouse about parking options in the vicinity.

» Info

You can find the most up-to-date parking information on www.visitbruges.be

▶ Parking Centrum-Station

Stationsplein | City map: D13
CAPACITY > 1500
OPEN > Daily, 24 hours a day
PRICE > Maximum €3.50/24 hrs | hourly rate: €0.70 | including free bus transfer (max. 4 people per car)

▶ Parking Centrum-'t Zand

Underneath 't Zand | City map: C9
CAPACITY > 1400
OPEN > Daily, 24 hours a day
PRICE > Maximum €8.70/24 hrs | hourly rate: €1.20; from the second hour you pay per quarter hour

🜂 Police

» General telephone number
tel. +32 (0)50 44 88 44
» Emergency police assistance   tel. 101
» Working hours
Monday to Friday: 8.00 a.m.-5.00 p.m. and Saturdays: 9.00 a.m.-6.00 p.m. you can contact the central police services at Kartuizerinnenstraat 4 | City map: E9
Daily: from 6.00 a.m. to 10.00 p.m. you can contact the railway police in the main NMBS train station | City map: C/D13
» After working hours
For urgent police assistance, there is a 24/7 service (contact by telephone) at the police station at the Lodewijk Coiseaukaai 3 | City map: F1

Post office

Smedenstraat 57-59 | City map: B9

You can also make use of one of the post points (advice, dispatch, stamps, etc.) or stamp shops (stamps only) that you can find in several of the shopping streets.

Public holidays

Belgium has quite a lot of public holidays. On these holidays most companies, shops, offices and public services are closed.

» 1 January (New Year's Day)
» 1 April (Easter Sunday)
   and 2 April (Easter Monday)
» 1 May (Labour Day)
» 10 May (Ascension Day)
» 20 May (Whit Sunday)
   and 21 May (Whit Monday)
» 11 July (Flemish regional holiday)
» 21 July (Belgian national holiday)
» 15 August (Assumption of Mary)
» 1 November (All Saints' Day)
» 11 November (Armistice Day)
» 25 December (Christmas)
» 26 December (Boxing Day)

Public transport

You can find the most up-to-date travel information on www.visitbruges.be

▶ 🚌 Bus

Public transport in Bruges is well organised. Buses run every five minutes between the station and the city centre. There are also frequent services to the train station and the city centre running from the bus stop for tourist buses at the Kanaaleiland ('canal Island'; City map: E13). The buses going to the city centre stop within easy walking distance of the main shopping streets, historical buildings and museums. The most important bus stops are marked on the city map (see the folding map on the inside of the back cover). A ticket allows you to change bus services as many times as you want for a period of 60 minutes. The ticket price is

€3. All De Lijn tickets can be bought at the following points of sale.

▶ Tickets
» Advance sales offices
De Lijnwinkel, Stationsplein
Tourist office on 🛈 't Zand
(Concert Hall)
Various book stores, newsagents and supermarkets in the city centre
» Vending machines De Lijn
De Lijnwinkel, Stationsplein
Bus stop 't Zand

Scooter rental

» 🛵 Electric Scooters
Rental of electric scooters (max. speed: 25 kph).
LOCATION > Gentpoortstraat 55 and 62
PRICE PER SCOOTER > 2 hours: €35; 4 hours: €50; full day: €65
OPEN > 1/4 to 31/10: Mondays, 1.00 p.m.-6.00 p.m.; Tuesdays to Saturdays, 10.00 a.m.-6.00 p.m.
CONDITIONS > Minimum age of driver = 23 years
EXTRA > Rental of electric bikes *(see page 150)*
INFO > Tel. +32 (0)50 61 16 46 and +32 (0)475 94 20 02, www.electric-scooters.be

» 🛵 Vespa Tours
LOCATION > Estaminet 't Molenhuis, Potterierei 109
PRICE PER VESPA > Including helmet and insurance, 1/2 day: €50 (1 person) or €65 (2 people); full day: €70 (1 person) or €80 (2 people)
OPEN > 1/3 to 1/10: daily, 10.00 a.m.-6.00 p.m.
CONDITIONS > Minimum age of driver = 21 years, driver's license B
EXTRA > Guided tours *(see page 142)*
INFO > Tel. +32 (0)497 64 86 48, www.vespatours-brugge.be

» 🛵 Vesparoute
LOCATION > Fietsverhuur B-Bike, Concert Hall, 't Zand

PRICE PER VESPA > Including helmet, insurance and petrol, 1/2 day (only possible Monday to Friday, 10.00 a.m.-2.00 p.m. or 2.00 p.m.-6.00 p.m.): €50 (1 person) or €60 (2 people); full day: €79 (1 person) or €89 (2 people)
OPEN > 1/4 to 31/10: daily, 10.00 a.m.-7.00 p.m.
CONDITIONS > Minimum age of driver = 21 years, driver's license B
INFO > Tel. +32 (0)479 97 12 80 or +32 (0)474 55 34 45, www.vesparoute.com

The company renting out the scooters usually requires the payment of a security deposit before departure.

Smoking

In Belgium there is a general ban on smoking in cafés, restaurants, public areas in hotels (lobby, bar, corridors, etc.) and in all public buildings (train stations, airports, etc.). Those unable to kick the habit will usually find an ashtray just outside.

Swimming pools
11 Interbad
Six 25-meter lanes; also a recreational pool, water slide, toddler's pool and teaching pool.
INFO > Veltemweg 35, Sint-Kruis, tel. +32 (0)50 35 07 77, interbad@skynet.be, www.interbad.be; scheduled bus no. 10, no. 58 or no. 58S, bus stop: Watertoren

12 Jan Guilini
25-meter indoor pool in a beautiful listed building, named after the swimming champion and resistance fighter Jan Guilini.
INFO > Keizer Karelstraat 41, tel. +32 (0)50 31 35 54, zwembadjanguilini@brugge.be, www.brugge.be/sport; scheduled bus no. 9, bus stop: Visartpark

13 📶 S&R Olympia
An Olympic size pool (50 metres), with a wide range of recreational facilities in a

'sub-tropical swimming paradise' (including slides, a wave pool, a wild-water run) and an outdoor sunbathing area (with two outdoor pools and several attractions).
INFO > Doornstraat 110, Sint-Andries, tel. +32 (0)50 67 28 70, olympia@sr-olympia.be, www.sr-olympia.be; scheduled bus no. 5, bus stop: Lange Molen or no. 25, bus stop: Jan Breydel

All information about opening times is available at the tourist office 🛈 Markt (Historium), 't Zand (Concert Hall) or Stationsplein (railway station).

Taxis

🚗 TAXI STANDS

» At Bruges station: city centre side and Sint-Michiels side
» At the Bargeweg (Kanaaleiland)
» On the Markt
» In the Vlamingstraat (opposite the City Theatre)
» In the Boeveriestraat (near 't Zand)
» In the Kuipersstraat (next to the library)

PRICE > The local taxi companies all use the same fixed-rate tariffs (adjustments are possible throughout the year):

Bruges <> Brussels Airport-Zaventem: €200
Bruges <> Brussels South Charleroi Airport: €250
Bruges <> Aéroport de Lille: €140
Bruges <> Ostend-Bruges Airport: €70
Bruges <> Brussels (city centre): €175
Bruges <> Zeebrugge: €50

You can find a list of licensed taxi companies on www.visitbruges.be

Telephones

If you want to phone someone in Bruges from abroad, you must first dial the country code (00)32, followed by the zone code 50, and the number of the person you want to contact. To phone Bruges from within Belgium, you dial 050 plus the number of the person.

Toilets

There are a number of public toilets in Bruges (see [wc] the fold-out plan at the back of the guide). Some are accessible for people with a disability. When local people need to use a toilet, they often pop into a cafe or pub to order something small so that they can use the facilities there.

🛈 📶 ♿ Tourist offices

There are three tourist information offices in Bruges.

» Tourist office Markt (Historium)
Daily, 10.00 a.m.-5.00 p.m.
» Tourist office 't Zand (Concert Hall)
Monday to Saturday, 10.00 a.m.-5.00 p.m.; Sundays and public holidays, 10.00 a.m.-2.00 p.m.

» Tourist office Railway Station (corridor to the platforms, city centre side)
Daily, 10.00 a.m.-5.00 p.m.

All tourist offices are closed on Christmas Day and New Year's Day. Tel. +32 (0)50 44 46 46, visitbruges@brugge.be, www.visitbruges.be

Travelling season and climate

Although most visitors come to the city in the spring and summer months, Bruges has something to offer all year round. The misty months of autumn and winter are ideal for atmospheric strolls along the canals and the cobbled streets, before ending up in a cosy restaurant or cheerful pub. Ambiance guaranteed, although every now and then you may have to put up with a little rain, so make sure you bring an umbrella! The 'cold' months are also perfect for undisturbed visits to the city's many museums and sites of interest, before again finishing up in one of those same restaurants or pubs! What's more, in January, February, March and often on weekdays as well, you can get great discounts on many accommodation outlets in Bruges.

Index of street names